HANDBOOK OF DEMAND PLANNING

Jay Sharma,
United Kingdom.

HANDBOOK OF DEMAND PLANNING

Note to the Reader

Over the last few years I have seen many companies ask the same questions and go through the same learning process to strive towards a 'Best Practice' Demand Planning Process.

One of the things that made this harder to achieve, has been the relative lack of books with basic practical knowledge of Demand Planning. All the texts I saw were either academic, software focussed, focussed on statistical forecasting or were covering a broader subject with Demand Planning just a short chapter in it. Various Software Vendors and consultants have publications, but they are mostly focussed on trying to sell or implement their products and services.

I have tried to put this book together in easy to read chapters focussed on giving basic knowledge to the Demand Planning Professional. The book covers and explains the basic principles and approaches in Demand Planning, specifically as applicable to the Manufacturing industry, but most sections can be applied to other industries as well.

I have tried to keep the focus of the book on business process and planning activities rather than on forecasting or IT systems. Also, to keep the book generic and non-biased, there is no mention or focus in the book of any specific Software or Application, even though we discuss generic ways of how they are structured and used.

I plan to update the book regularly and release new versions with additional chapters, examples and modifications.

Lastly, if you want to get this book customised for your company with your own examples, business scenarios, images and terminology please drop a mail to jay.sharma@supplychainpro.co.uk

Jay Sharma

Comments, suggestions and contributions are welcome and will be incorporated in updated versions if suitable and acknowledged. Enquiries for customization or corporate requirements may be forwarded for quotes. Training and Consulting engagement queries are welcome. Please address all communication to the email address below.

Jay.Sharma@SupplychainPro.co.uk

Table of Contents

HANDBOOK OF DEMAND PLANNING

Chapter 1

What is a Supply Chain?

A Supply Chain consists of all activities involved in fulfilling a customer's requirement. The Supply Chain includes, not only Retail Manufacturing and suppliers but also transporters, warehouses and the customers themselves.

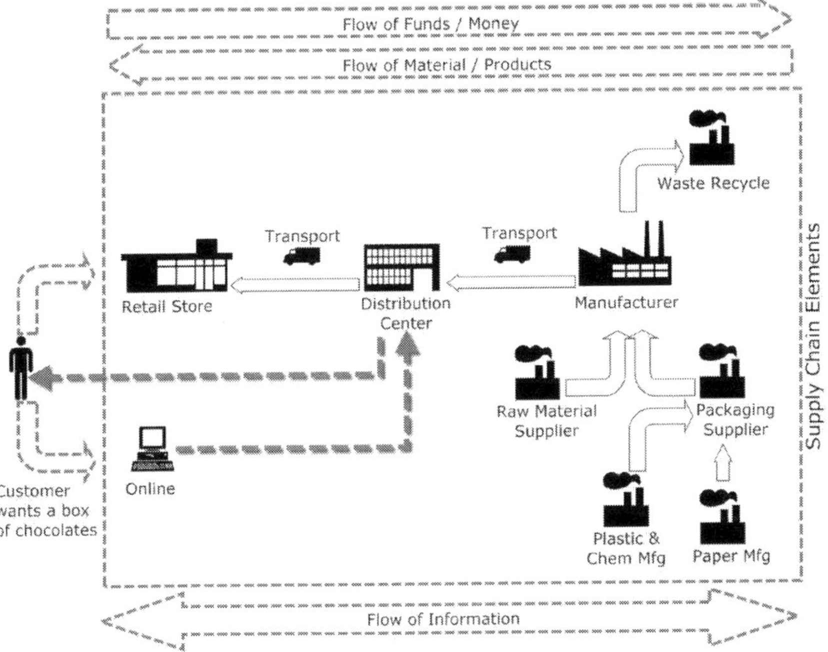

An Organization's Supply Chain includes all functions involved in filling its own customers' requirements. These may not be the final end consumers of your product. In the example above a customer needing to buy a box of chocolates may decide to either buy it from a retail store or place an order online. The Retail Store is serviced from a DC / Warehouse which holds stocks against expected demand. The DC/Warehouse is supplied by the manufacturer and may hold multiple types of products .The Manufacturer of the chocolate box of course has its own suppliers of Raw Materials and Packing Material. The Packing Material Supplier may source its Raw Materials from other Plastic and Paper manufacturing companies who may be recycling materials or sourcing chemicals and Timber from other companies. The whole network of relationships works towards anticipating and fulfilling the customer's requirement (which in this example is a box of chocolates) and are part of a Supply Chain.

A Supply Chain involves the constant flow of:

- Products and Materials (From Suppliers to Customers)
- Funds and Cash (From Customers to Suppliers)
- Information (Both ways)

The Customer is the origin of all Demand even though some supply chain partners may not have complete visibility of it.

Supply Chain Decisions

Every organization needs to make multiple decisions related to its Supply Chain. These can be grouped into three categories based on the importance and impact of the decisions:

Supply Chain Strategic Decisions – These decisions are usually related to the structure and design of supply chains, for example:

- Structure of the Distribution network
- Geographical coverage
- Transportation Modes
- Manufacturing capacity
- Sourcing / Outsourcing
- Merge, close or open new locations, DCs, Manufacturing facilities

Strategic decisions usually involve heavy capital investment and are typically made with long term objectives in mind (e.g. five years or more depending on industry).

Supply Chain Planning Decisions – These decisions drive the short and medium term operations of an organization:

- Forecasting / Demand Planning
- Inventory policy and stock levels
- Promotions
- Manufacturing levels
- Defining Priority in constrained supply scenarios
- New Product Introduction

Planning decisions are constrained within the Strategic Decisions, which cover the Long term Horizon. These decisions usually involve SKU and SKU Group level planning with an objective of maximising revenue and volumes within a financial year.

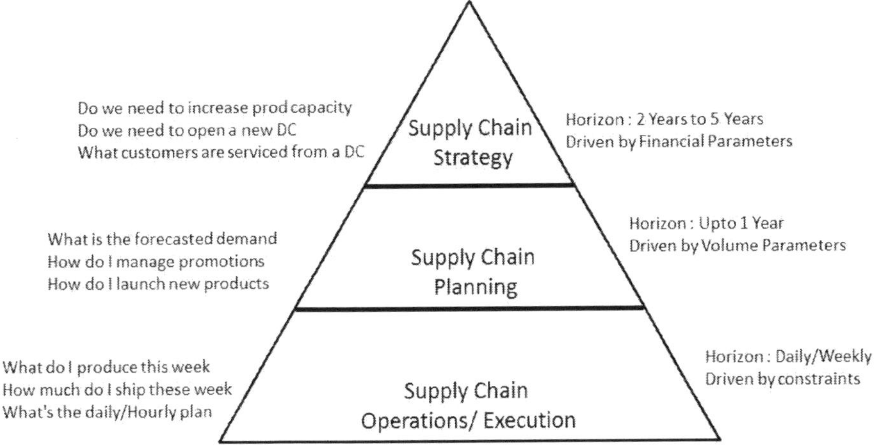

Supply Chain Operational Decisions – These decisions are usually related to servicing immediate customer needs, immediate term production decisions and current inventory deployment:

- Manufacturing – Hourly/ Daily decisions
- Stock Deployment
- Servicing Customer orders
- Manufacturing Mix changes

- Ship current stock

Operational decisions usually involve changes in the immediate and short term (Typically a day to a week).

Push Vs. Pull Decisions

Supply Chain processes can be categorised into two types, depending on their relation to Customer Demand.

Pull Type Processes: In Pull processes, the supply chain reacts in response to a Customer Order. Here the exact demand is known but the supply chain usually has a short window to react to fulfil it. Long term visibility of customer orders is usually rare and the variability high. Production manufactures only what is ordered. A pull system is meant to produce higher customer satisfaction, lower inventory and a constantly changing product design to meet changing customers' needs. Pull processes are sometimes also called Customer Centric as the emphasis is on Customer Orders and needs.

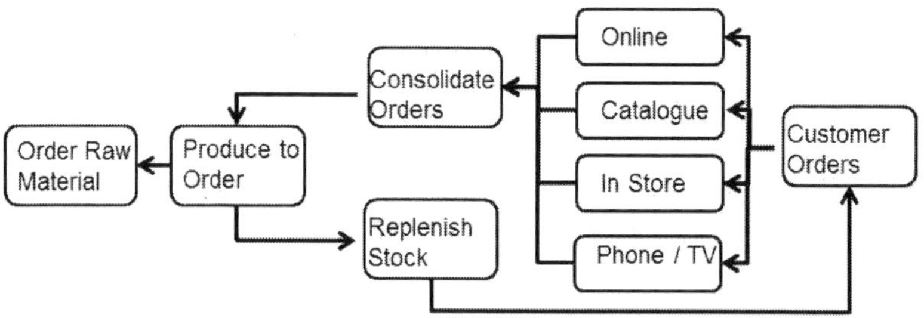

Push Type Processes: In Push processes, the supply chain manufactures and stocks goods in anticipation of customer orders (or forecasted demand).

The company can build to forecasted demand, but carries the risk of higher inventory costs, finished goods obsolescence and slow response to customer changes. These costs are expected to be offset against faster access to customers, higher inventory turnover and increased efficiencies of manufacturing and sourcing.

Push processes are sometimes also called Product Centric as the emphasis is on manufacturing and stocking products based on a company's internal decisions. The push system is more effective in dealing with fluctuating demand. Producers can store finished products in anticipation of demand, even though this incurs an inventory cost, or they can create additional demand by focussing on selling products that have already been produced.

Product **Push** through the Supply Chain

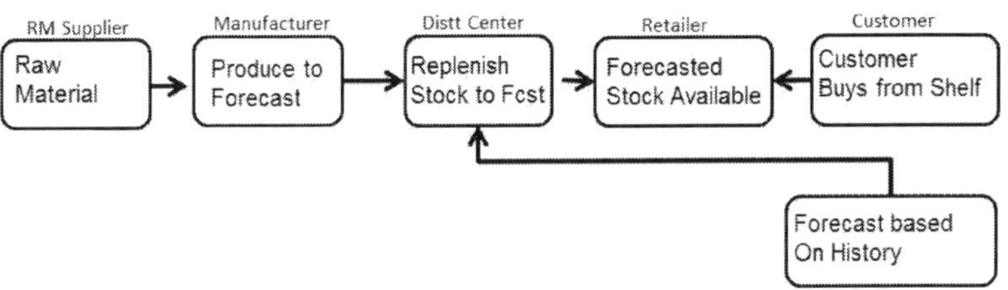

The push/pull boundary can be imagined as the point in a supply chain beyond which demand is fulfilled through stock in the supply chain. As an example for a retailer, Should the company directly replenish the stores from suppliers? Or, should the company replenish the stores from a distribution centre that stocks inventory and gets replenished from suppliers, Or should the company have A National Distribution centre to service multiple smaller Distribution Centres. In case the stores are directly replenished by orders placed on the suppliers, the company may save on the warehousing costs but carry higher distribution costs and risk of stockouts. In the second (and third) case, the company consolidates its stocks at a single distribution centre and reduces its stockout risk, but increases its inventory and warehousing costs.

In all off these scenarios, the company is engaged in a trade-off between balancing the cost of inventory against the customer service levels.

The following criteria may be used as guidelines in deciding Push vs. Pull approach within a supply chain:

- **Demand Variability**: When the product demand is stable, and can be forecasted with relatively high accuracy, a push strategy is indicated. When demand uncertainty is high, consider pull strategies for managing demand. Low demand variability provides an opportunity to create highly efficient manufacturing or distribution processes that may not be very flexible but minimize the cost of unit production. High demand variability works against such efficiencies.

- **Product Variability**: The products that are customized and typically require personalization at the consumer level will do well with a pull strategy for effective demand management. However, the fulfilment lead-time must be managed to be competitive.

- **Economies of Scale**: The product characteristics described above generally also describe the economies of scale. With manufacturing based on large economies of scale (and hence no or low customization), push strategies are generally beneficial.

- **Manufacturing Setup Changes**: When the manufacturing setup changes are expensive and time-consuming, a push-based strategy should be evaluated. Consider pull strategies when setup changes are quick and do not affect the manufacturing efficiencies substantially.

- **Lead-time**: Lead-time in this context means the lead-time to fulfil demand. This can be replenishment, manufacturing, or distribution lead-time or a combination of these, depending on the specific situation. Higher lead-time generally favours push-systems to build inventory so that end-demand can be fulfilled relatively quickly.

The push/pull decisions afford a balance between the responsiveness (agility) and cost (lean). Pull systems must be responsive to be effective. Push systems are generally more cost effective though they not have the same amount of flexibility as the pull-systems may have.

Pull	Push
☐ Trigger : Customer Order	☐ Trigger : Demand Forecast
☐ Reactive	☐ Anticipative
☐ High Demand Variability	☐ Low Demand Variability
☐ High Customisation	☐ Low Manufacturing Variability
☐ Low FG Inventory	☐ High FG Inventory
☐ High Lead Times	☐ Low/ No Lead Time

In reality, for most companies, there is always a mix of Push and Pull processes as they may have confirmed customer orders for the short term but will have to work with forecasted demand based on history, for medium and long term purpose. Deciding whether a particular supply chain is push or pull based is often difficult, and generally depends on the perspective of what constitutes the supply chain and where particular participants are placed in the chain. Companies may also change from a Pull to Push approach from time to time, in reaction to market forces and competitor strategies. The Push or Pull strategy of a company may also be supported by relevant trade promotions or consumer targeted activities and pricing decisions. Lastly, the decision to follow Push or Pull (or a hybrid) strategy is usually a long term strategic decision outside the one to two year horizon, depending on the type of industry.

Supply Chains and Demand Chains

A recent development has been the concept of Demand Chains (as opposed to Supply Chains). The term Supply Chain implied a 'Push' approach, where the focus was on manufacturing, distributing and retailing products out to satisfy forecasted demand.

A Demand Chain on the other hand implies that the focus is on the customer and it's the customer demand, which pulls the stock and products through the whole network. The difference between supply chains and Demand chains is down to the Push and Pull decisions discussed earlier.

It should be noted that most companies still use the term Supply Chain and it's the more commonly used term, irrespective of the nature of decision making within an organization.

The role of Demand Planning

The Demand Planning role becomes very important in case of Push Type Supply Chains. In this case the Forecast becomes the demand trigger and drives the whole supply chain planning process, Short Term as well as Long Term.

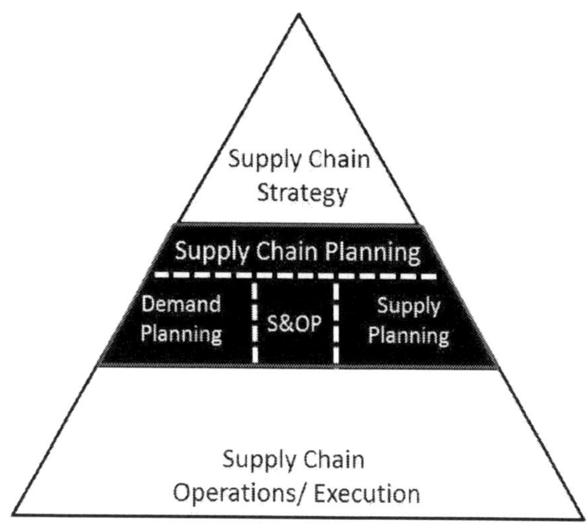

The Demand Planning function is a key component of the Supply Chain Planning layer of decision making. It should be considered as a part of the planning team interfacing with Marketing, Sales, Production, Merchandising, Sourcing and Finance (wherever relevant). In the best organizational structures, the Demand Planning Function is not a part of any one of the above departments and cuts across all of the above. It's however, common to find Demand Planning teams reporting into Sales and Marketing in companies that are strongly driven by sales or Marketing. A typical organization structure may look as below:

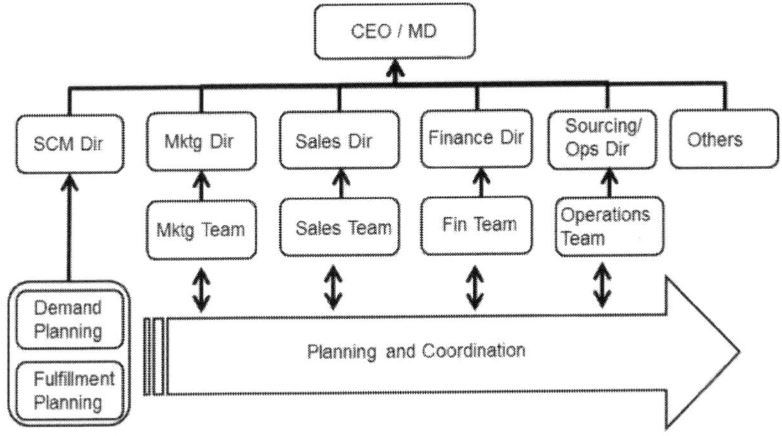

The role of Demand Planning assumes a key role depending on the Customer Lead Time (time the customer will wait for his needs to be fulfilled) and the Supply Chain Lead Time (time taken by your supply chain to fulfil the customer needs).

The longer your customers lead time is compared to your supply chain lead time, the less of a role Demand Planning plays in your business.

As this difference shortens, Demand Planning starts playing a key role, especially when the Customer lead Time is zero (as in the case of Retail) or much shorter than the Supply Chain Lead time (e.g. FMCG).

Thought Points……. .

- [ ] Draw the end to end Supply Chain network for your company.
  Who is the final customer of your Supply Chain Network.
  Where does your company sit in the Network

- [ ] What are the different Supply Chain Decisions that impact your Companies operations. Group them into the different decision levels.
  What decisions do you directly impact.

- [ ] Is your Supply Chain a Push or Pull type (or a Push/Pull Hybrid).
  What drives demand in your Supply Chain.
  What would happen if you changed the Demand Trigger.

- [ ] How is your Supply Chain Team structured.
  Who does your Demand Planning Team report into
  How does your Demand Planning team work with other Departments.

notes..................

notes.................

Chapter 2

What is Demand Planning?

The Demand Planning processes equal a collection of steps with a single goal in mind: to deliver a single demand plan by item and location (or customer) that will drive both financial and sales planning processes, downstream inventory planning and operational processes. It is an iterative process that runs at regular intervals (usually once per week). The output is a time-phased forecast for the planning horizon (usually a year or two years, but can be more).

The Demand Planning process may include a set of business processes, which define the following:

- Management of demand history as it comes into your supply chain planning systems.
- Introduction and Management of New Products/SKUs.
- Addition/revision of existing SKU data, product hierarchies and maps for aggregation of history and forecast.
- Creation of the Base Statistical Forecast.
- Application of Promotions Forecast, impact of events and other Forecast based on planner judgement.
- Creation of the Total Sales Forecast incorporating all elements of Demand.
- Resolution of business and statistical exceptions.
- Demand Planning Consensus process.
- Tracking and monitoring of forecast results.

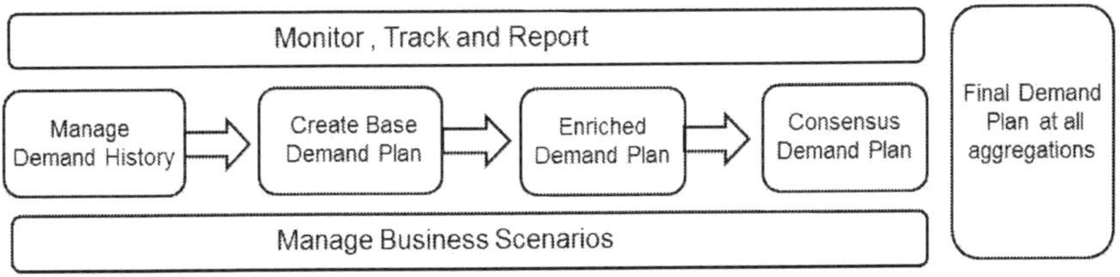

Success Factors for Demand Planning

The critical Success factors for Demand Planning are:

- The Demand Plan must provide a single source of consistent information on anticipated product demand.
- The accuracy of the Demand Plan must be measured and understood.
- The Demand Forecast must be based on objective, realistic and visible assumptions, which are under regular review.
- The Demand Forecast must be derived through consensus with other teams' plans. (E.g. Financial Plans, Top Down plans etc.).
- There must be an established timetable for developing the plan that includes sign-off by the identified owners of the plan.
- Constraints on meeting the Demand Forecast must be accurately reflected in the Demand Plan and clearly recorded.
- Short Term Demand Plan must be clearly identified and treated separately from the Long Term Demand Plan.
- The Demand Planning function should be treated as a team coordinating with all concerned departments, rather than one that sits within the team of a single department.
- The highest stakeholders in the organization should recognize the importance of Demand Planning.
- The Demand Planning activities should be supported by systems and tools as fit the company's processes and technological architecture.
- There should be regular training, education and cross-pollination of ideas within the Demand Planning community in the organization.
- The Demand Planning solution should be integrated with Supply and supply chain execution systems.
- The Demand Planning process should be exception driven and focussed on the areas that add most value to the company's business.

The scope of Demand Planning

The Demand Planning process is an integral part of the planning process for any Manufacturer or Retailer.

The output of the Demand Planning process is a Demand Forecast, which may be split by Base Forecast and Market Intelligence. The Base Forecast reflects the normal demand for a product and the Market Intelligence reflects the additional demand generated by the company's internal efforts (sales, marketing and promotions).A further tweaking of the Forecast may be done for uncontrollable external factors and one off events.

A standard approach is to generate the demand plans on a weekly basis, and engage in a weekly collaborative effort within the demand planning team to finalise the forecast. This is then used for prioritising and planning around supply constraints in coordination with the Supply/Operations teams.

On a Monthly basis there should be a meeting of the larger group of stakeholders (Finance, Sales, Marketing, Demand and Supply) in a Sales & Operations Planning (S&OP) meeting to resolve conflicts and constrain the Demand Plan based on inputs from other teams.

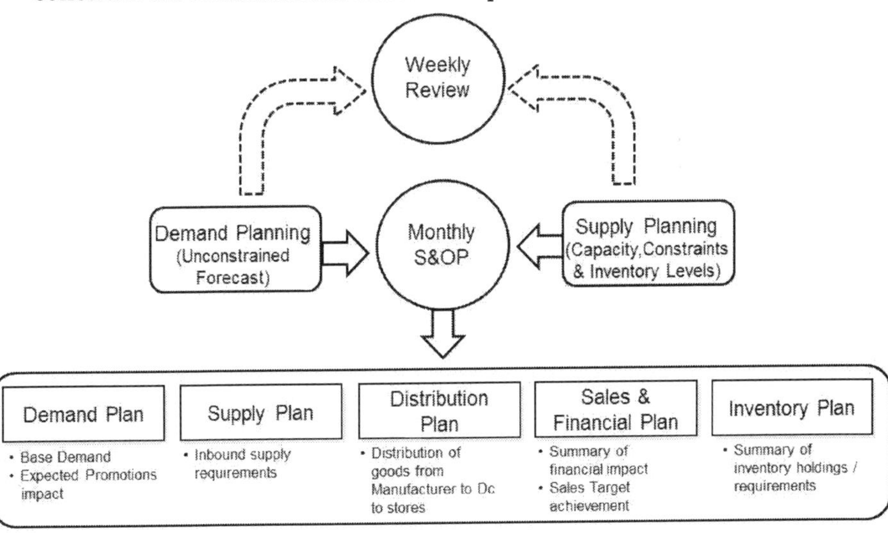

High Level Demand Planning Process

The Demand Planning process starts with History. On a regular basis incremental sales history is loaded. This is analysed and adjusted if necessary. In addition, any new SKUs and any changes to existing SKUs are brought into the planning system.

The base statistical forecast is then created based on the updated history in the system and the exceptions to the base forecast resolved.

Market intelligence is then added to the Base Forecast based on input from various teams (sales, marketing etc.) as well as the Planners judgement and the organizational ways of working.

The demand plan is then subjected to a Demand Consensus process where all the contributors to the Forecast agree on a final number. The forecast that has been agreed upon by all parties with a stake in the forecast is then published to supply, operations and finance.

The forecast performance is constantly monitored and tracked to gain visibility of forecast related metrics.

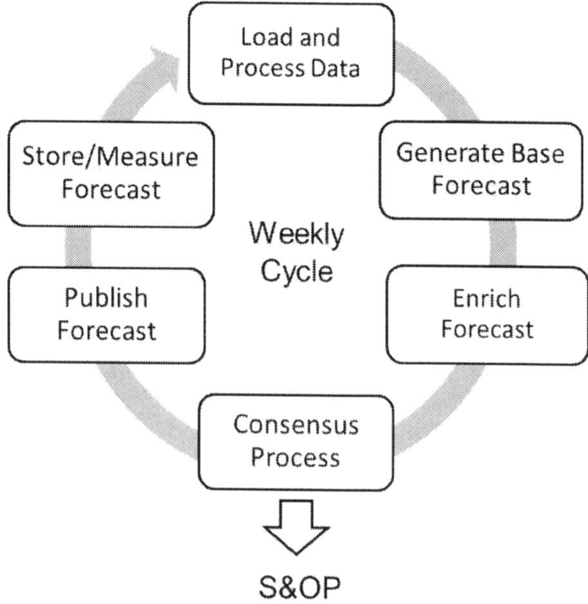

Demand Planning Process Steps

The Demand Planner doesn't have to do all steps in the demand planning process manually, and usually a company will have Demand Planning systems and software to perform a majority of these steps. As we shall see later, the Demand Planners role then becomes one of monitoring and adding value with his inputs. Lets look the steps given above in some more detail:

Step 1: Load and Process Data: This may happen once a week for data in weekly buckets or Daily for companies planning Demand on a Daily basis (some companies may do this monthly). The source data is usually your ERP or Order Management Systems, with interfaces configured to extract specified data and populate your Demand Planning System.

The sub processes and activities under this step are:

- Aggregation and Loading of History data automatically (Daily data aggregated to weekly or monthly time bucket).
- Data may be filtered for specified data conditions (e.g. negative history for returns)
- New products setup in your Demand Planning system, triggered by input from your ERP systems.
- Additional Data / Factors may be loaded along with the History if they are expected to have an impact on demand (assuming your Demand Planning system supports the data). This could be prices, temperature, stockout, promotions or other relevant data.
- Updations to existing MasterData in your Demand Planning solution, triggered by MasterData changes in your ERP setup (e.g. product Hierarchy changes etc.).

Once the Initial Data is setup the planners should then be able to perform the following (if required):

- Manually adjust History for outliers, incorrect data or simple mistakes.

- Perform any activities needed to start planning for new products (this is covered in detail in a later section).
- Import any forecast that has been supplied by the customers into your Demand Planning system. This could also be customer orders.

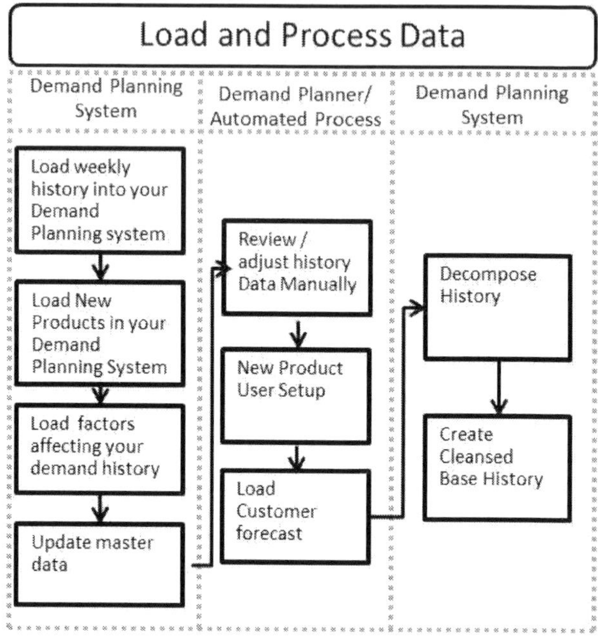

The Demand planning System will then , usually take the input data and the user added changes and performs the next two steps.

- Decompose the history into its various elements. Separately identify the promotions impact and user identified anomalies and outliers from the Base History. This is usually an automated process within most Demand Planning Systems, but the extent of decomposition may differ based on which systems you use.
- Create a history data stream of cleansed History Data which models just the base history without the impact of other events, promotions etc. The base History may be adjusted for additional

factors like stockouts by your Demand Planning system. At this stage we may want to exclude some SKUs from History cleansing if the history is short or patchy.

Its common for a company to skip some of the steps above, based on how its Demand Planning System is setup. Some Demand Planning systems actually store the cleansed history at this stage while others get the same results using parameters (without storing the cleansed History).

Step 2: Generate Base Forecast: The next step in the demand planning process leads to the creation of Base Forecast.

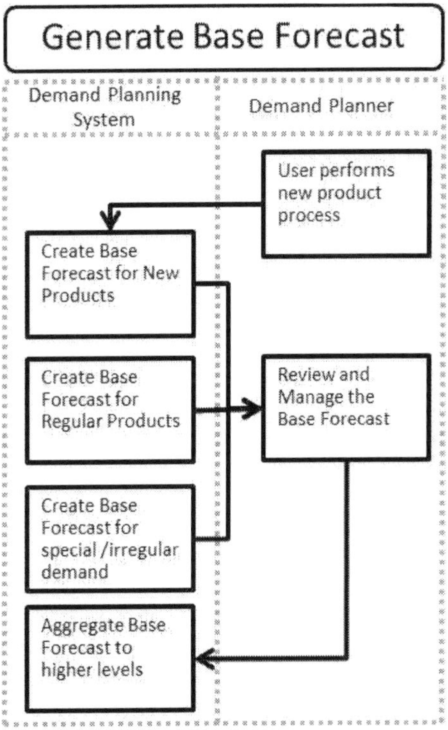

The sub processes and activities under this step are explained below:

- The planner may be required to perform additional steps to ensure base forecast is created for New Products.
- Most Demand Planning Systems would also support new product forecasting and would at this stage create artificial base forecast for new products based on inputs from Planners. For example an input could be, the average expected sales for the new product.
- At the same time your Demand Planning Solution would also be expected to generate base forecast using the cleansed Base

History for most of your regular products. Separate algorithms and parameters are usually employed to generate a forecast for irregular products / products that are sold sporadically.

- The Planners may then tweak the parameters and regenerate the forecast before they are satisfied with it. The best Demand Planning systems usually support this with an exception management process to guide the planners with exception messages and alerts. Some of the Demand Planning Solutions may also allow customised exception messages to be created.
- Lastly the Base Forecast for all products is aggregated to Higher Levels, in case forecasting is done at multiple levels within the company.

Step 3: Enrich Forecast: Once the base forecast has been created for all products, the planner can then enrich the forecast by adding inputs from Sales and Marketing. He could also add and modify forecast based on his experience and business scenarios specific to his company.

Note: Base History and Base Forecast in this text represent regular demand for a product after removing the impact of promotions, one off events or external factors.

The sub processes and activities under this step are explained below:

- At this stage the planner can add uplifts to the base forecast for future sales promotions and marketing campaigns. This usually done based on input from the Sales and Marketing teams and will either be added manually, imported or generated within your Demand planning systems based on the solutions in place.
- Additional Sales and Marketing input may be applied for a downlift impact due to cannibalization of volumes by a promotion.

- Sometimes the sales and marketing estimates may be provided at an aggregate level instead of SKU Level. In such cases they need to be added at an aggregate level forecast before their impact is split down to SKU level. This is usually done by apportioning the volumes based on Historical ratios or ratios of base forecast at SKU Level.
- Forecast for New Products is generated either by copying History, applying lifecycles or manual inputs.
- Sales Targets may be applied to fix the Forecast to a certain level, based on agreements with customers or Targets agreed by sales (even though the trend predicts different volumes).
- Top-down adjustments may be applied based on management decisions around the product portfolio and strategic market focus. These are usually applied at aggregate levels and their impact trickled down.
- Lastly the Total Forecast is summarised at the SKU Level after taking into account the impact of all forecast changes and market intelligence gathered by the Demand Planners at all aggregate levels..

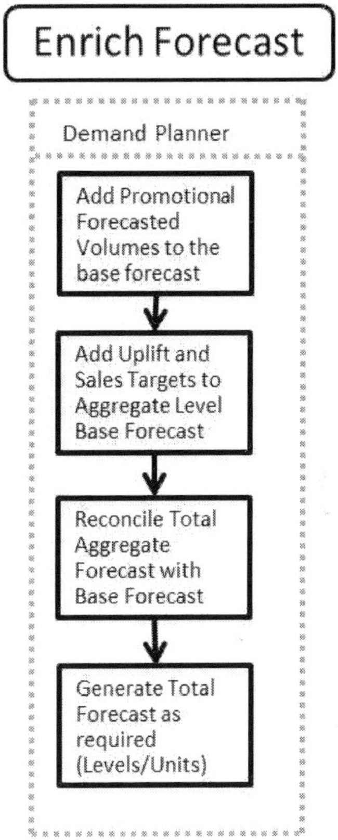

Enrich Forecast

Demand Planner

Add Promotional Forecasted Volumes to the base forecast

↓

Add Uplift and Sales Targets to Aggregate Level Base Forecast

↓

Reconcile Total Aggregate Forecast with Base Forecast

↓

Generate Total Forecast as required (Levels/Units)

An important requirement during forecast enrichment step is to ensure that all changes are transparent and visible to people reviewing forecasts. Advanced systems will also give you the capability to audit and maintain change logs indicating why and who made changes to the statistical forecast.

Review of Steps 1 to 3

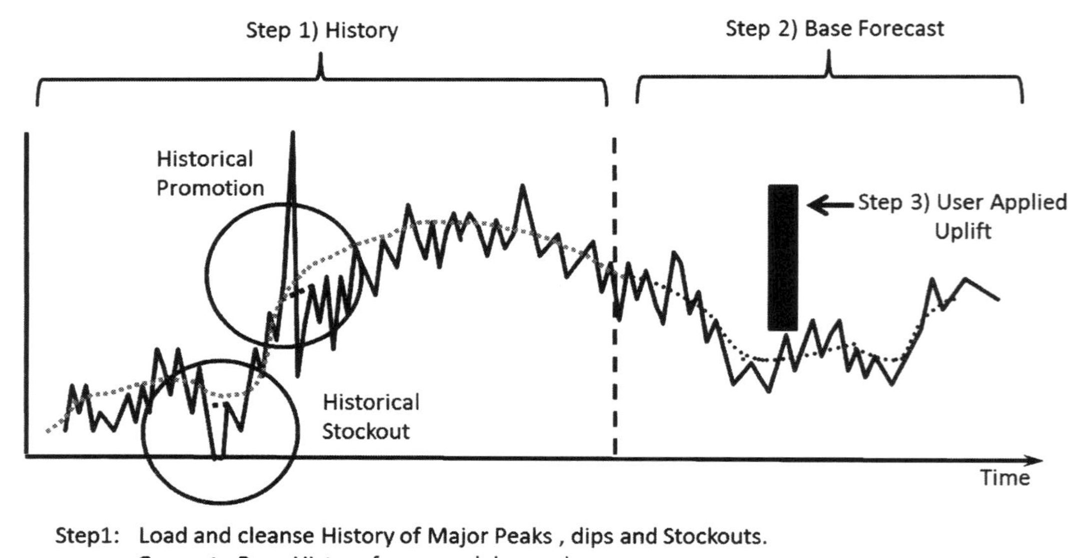

Step1: Load and cleanse History of Major Peaks , dips and Stockouts.
Generate Base History for normal demand.

Step 2: Generate Base Forecast for Normal Demand using Base History.
User scenarios for Managing Base Forecast for exceptional SKU's.

Step 3: User applies uplift to base forecast for Promotions , sales targets etc.
User reconciles forecasts at aggregate and SKU levels in case of multi-level forecasting.

Step 4: Consensus Process: Once the Total forecast has been created after incorporating inputs from Sales and Marketing, the planner should maintain the Forecast through an iterative consensus process on a weekly basis. This would be an internal alignment and updation of the Forecast as the timeline moves forward. This would also cover any pre-S&OP meeting requirements and weekly updates into the S&OP data if required. The final stage of the consensus process is when all the key stakeholders come together in an S&OP meeting to agree to the demand plan based on constraints and other considerations.

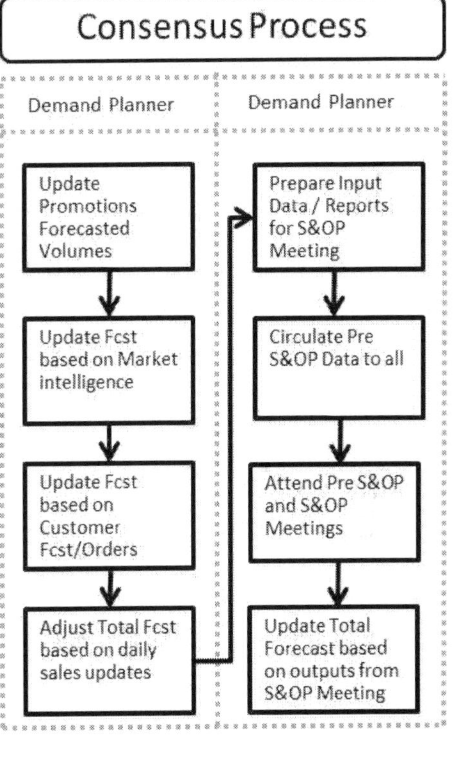

The sub processes and activities under this step are explained below:

- The planner updates the forecast on a regular basis, based on changing inputs from Sales and Marketing regarding expected uplifts during promotions and marketing campaigns. This may happen because of changed Market Mix, changes to Marketing Campaigns, changes to Trade Allowances or feedback from end customers.
- The Total Forecast is adjusted and agreed with Marketing and sales before the Planner creates input data and reports for the S&OP Meeting.
- The Planner then attends the S&OP Meeting with detailed data, provides his inputs and suggestions and at the end of the

meeting, and updates the Total Forecast based on decisions made in the S&OP Meeting.

Note: The consensus process is also a key reason for companies to work at Weekly TimeBucket level. Daily Timebuckets and demand planning cycle is too short to give time for all parties to agree to a Consensus Forecast. Monthly Time buckets are too long and do not allow corrections within the S&OP cycle as most companies have a Monthly S&OP.

Step 5: Publish Forecast: At the end of the consensus process the Planner will usually publish his forecast to various parties and stakeholders.

The sub processes and activities under this step are:

- Final Forecast will be published to Supply / Operations for supply and operations planning which acts as the input to Production Plans.
- The Final Forecast will be sent out to suppliers as supplier orders in case the company does not manufacture but sources all the goods from suppliers.
- The Final Forecast may be shared with customers to make them aware of the future demand plans.
- The Final Forecast may also be shared with internal parties for reporting, input into financial planning, computation of trade allowances, long term planning and product mix and promotions decisions.
- The Final Forecast is published at the end of a week in case of a weekly planning cycle.
- Published Forecast is usually considered for any Forecast Accuracy calculations.
- In some cases Forecast may be published more than once a week if your planning requirements in other areas (supply, Finance etc.) don't fall on the same day.

- Forecast is published only for the forecast agreed and finalised. This may or may not be for all products.

Step 6: Store/Measure Forecast: The last step of the planning cycle involves storing the Future Forecast over a defined horizon for analysis. This Forecast will later be compared against the actual History as it occurs to compute the forecast accuracy:

- The Forecast stored should be the Final Forecast after the consensus process.
- In case your products have supply side constraints, it makes sense to measure forecast accuracy in the same bucket as the S&OP Process. In such cases you can then store the constrained forecast after S&OP, to measure its forecast accuracy against actual history. Some companies may want to store a constrained Forecast and then measure its accuracy if they have major supply side constraints which don't allow them to fulfil the forecasted demand.
- Most Demand Planning systems will store forecast automatically after a period has closed. The frequency, duration and other parameters for storing forecasts are usually specified by a company depending on its requirements.
- Historical Forecast should stored at its lowest component level (Statistical Forecast and Planner added/changed components during the enrichment process) to enable reporting and measurement at Forecast Component level.
- The reporting of accuracy is usually done by separate Business Intelligence or reporting teams/software and not by the Demand Planners. These reports can either be at SKU level, aggregated levels or drill down reports where one can view lower level details.

Thought Points........

- ☐ chart out your demand planning process.
  How is your demand planning process linked to other planning processes in your company.

- ☐ What are History and Forecast Buckets.
  What could be factors deciding the time buckets to be used.
  Why is consensus important for the Demand Planning Process.

- ☐ What will happen if the History is not cleansed.
  Does History need to be cleansed of peaks for all SKUs.
  What is the difference between Base Forecast and Total Forecast.

- ☐ How important is the Planner in the Demand Planning Cycle.
  How important is Data in the Demand Planning Cycle.
  How important are Systems in the Demand Planning Cycle.

notes................

notes..............

Chapter 3

The Role of a Demand Planner

The Demand Planner performs a cross functional planning and coordinating role and the scope of his role may differ from company to company depending on how sales and operations are organized.

In working within the planning/supply chain department, the Planner helps to develop the "one number" forecast that is critical in achieving financial goals as well as improved customer service levels. The Demand Planner position requires an individual with a good understanding of the business environment as well as detailed knowledge of Demand Planning, Forecasting and Demand Planning Systems.

> Note: "one number" forecast means using a single source of SKU Level forecast for all planning activities within a company

Some of the responsibilities of a Demand Planner include: establish and maintain baseline statistical forecasts; work with management to identify trends, risks, new products, and new customers; review/resolve exceptions, work with Inventory Planners to track actual sales against forecasted sales; generate forecast performance reports etc. The Key Objectives for a Demand Planner are:

- Creation and maintenance of an accurate consensus forecast.
- Drive improvements to the Forecasting and demand planning process
- Operate the Demand Planning System used by the company.
- Balance of Sales, Marketing, Finance, Operations, Customer, and Supplier activities with a statistical forecast based on historical data to derive a consensus forecast
- Generate a One Number forecast for use by all key stakeholders

Sample Day-in-the-Life of a Demand Planner

Daily Activities

- Review / Resolve exceptions.
- Add Events/Uplifts.
- Setup New Products.
- Discontinue Products.
- History Data Cleansing.
- Review Forecasts for Key products.

Weekly Activities

- Review / Cleanse History
- Run Reports & Distribute
- Review Exceptions
- Update sales, product and market management, customer service and manufacturing with the new unconstrained forecast.
- Work with Supply Planner to create the demand plan and will be an member of the Sales, Operations, and Inventory Planning (SOIP) team
- Measure Forecast Accuracy and investigate reasons for poor forecast (if any).

Monthly Activities

- Facilitate Consensus (S&OP) Meeting
- Facilitate Product Launch Meeting
- Own the consensus forecast, which is the key input to distribution requirements planning , production planning etc
- Translates strategies of targeted markets and products into a long-term forecast and determine a long-term demand plan for the all production facilities.
- Manage the short & mid term forecast and modify to incorporate inputs and constraints from all key stakeholders.

Ad-Hoc Activities

- Transition New products to regular Products.
- Archive/ Delete History.
- Input Customer Forecast into planning systems.
- Maintain Aggregation Maps (If Any)
- Participate in Rollouts, Upgrades and implementations of your Demand Planning System.

Continuous

- Training / Workshops/ Continuous Learning.
- Support creation of standardised documents
- Support Process Template creation for rolling out the demand planning solution to other areas/regions
- Product/ customer segmentation analysis, forecast accuracy trends, business trends analysis, events/ issues affecting demand (causal effects, promotions, etc.), what-if analysis, and work with sales and marketing to quantify impact of business strategies/tactics, price increases/decreases, and new product introduction.

Daily Tasks

> **Note:** The Purpose of a "Day in the Life" document is to outline the typical activities and practices which should be followed by a Demand Planner.

The Demand Planner will usually have a daily schedule of activities to perform.

- Daily review of exceptions. This would usually be done on the days immediately after a planning cycle starts. For example , if the demand planning is done in weekly buckets and a week is defined as Monday to Sunday, exception resolution would usually be done on Monday or Tuesday after the weekly data has been loaded and forecast generated by the planning system.
- Once the exceptions are resolved the Planner can then perform setup for new and modified SKUs. He would also be expected to flag discontinued products for removal.
- A key daily task will be to cleanse the newly loaded History of Outliers, Events and Promotions effects. In some cases the system may do this automatically.
- Lastly the planner would review key/ critical products to ensure their forecast looked correct.

Weekly Tasks

The weekly tasks are usually performed once in a week by the Demand Planner.

- The Planner will share the base Forecast with Sales and Marketing and work collaboratively with then to gather and input future uplift volumes for promotions and events.
- The Planner will then publish the total forecast once a week to key stakeholders and update the S&OP plan if needed.
- Forecast accuracy and other Key Parameters will also be evaluated on a weekly basis when the weekly cycle has ended.
- The planner will also communicate exceptions and issues to appropriate levels in the organization.

Monthly Tasks

The Monthly tasks are usually for S&OP and constraint planning purposes and aligned with a company's S&OP Cycle.

- The Demand planner prepares input data and reports for the S&OP Meeting and circulates to all stakeholders before the meeting.
- The planner initiates and facilitates the New Product Meetings with Sales & Marketing.
- The Planner initiates and facilitates any other Pre-S&OP Meetings.
- The Planner participates in the S&OP Meeting. In case of multiple Demand Planners they would perform all of these tasks for separate categories/accounts/channels or Regions and then participate in the S&OP Meeting.
- At the end of the meeting the Planner goes away and updates the Forecast / constraints the forecast based on decisions and inputs from the S&OP Meeting.
- The Planner then owns the Forecast and manages it till the next S&OP Meeting.

Ad-Hoc & Continuous Tasks

These tasks are either one–off tasks, need based tasks or continuous tasks separate from the daily, weekly and monthly tasks.

- Initiates programs to improve Supply Chain Performance Indicators.
- Maintain professional and technical knowledge by attending educational workshop and conferences and reviewing professional publications.
- Reloading of History/ deletion of History if needed.
- Create new account/stores or regions.
- Create Year end comparison reports.
- Roll out your Demand Planning system to new locations / regions / countries.

Roles and Responsibilities Matrix

Task	Demand Planner	Marketing	Sales
Creates and monitors statistical baseline forecast	√		
Generates forecast performance reports at appropriate aggregations	√		
Contacts appropriate sources of information for issue resolution	√		
Contributes sales specific information to the forecast			√
Contributes the expected impact of marketing plans to the forecast		√	
Contributes the expected impact of sales promotions & initiatives to the forecast			√
Contributes information about competitors to the forecast		√	√
Contributes information about new products to the forecast	√	√	
Leads consensus meeting, facilitates conflict resolution	√		
Contributes long term sales targets and expectations to the forecast			√
Owns the forecast and makes final decisions within guidelines	√		

Some Challenges faced by Demand Planners

New Product Forecasting

Challenges:

- Large number of products being introduced regularly.
- Forecasting in the absence of History or other data.
- Inability to associate with like-items due to products being unique.

Possible Solutions:

- Copy History and other data from like-items.
- Create Manual forecast for the initial launch period and start generating forecast once enough history has been captured.

Short Life Cycles

Challenges:

- Products have very short life cycles, which means the planners don't have enough historical data to support robust forecasting.
- Workload increase as there is a lot of manual intervention and monitoring required.

Possible Solutions:

- Copy History and other data from like-items.
- Creating library of annual profiles and assign them to these products.

Adjustment for Stockouts

Challenges:

- Adjusting history for lost sales due to stockouts.

Possible Solutions:

- Maintain a record of periods when there is a stockout and replace that periods History with Average History.

History Cleansing

Challenges:

- History is usually not clean and heavily saturated with promotional influences and other events.
- Promotions and Base History not stored separately from total history for promoted periods.
- Uncleansed History Leading to poor forecasts.

Possible Solutions:

- Identify all major peaks, which are significantly higher than the average sale of a SKU and replace them with average SKU sale.
- Manually remove all major peaks as a one off exercise for historical promoted periods

Other Drivers of Demand

Challenges:

- Demand is usually impacted by other causal factors like Price/ Temperature / Store expansion etc.
- Historical data is usually not available for all causal factors
- These Causal factors may not impact all SKUs
- Future Causal Factor data may not be available

Possible Solutions:

- Start capturing Causal Factor data so that enough robust data is available in the near future.
- If the data is available, test their effect on demand using a small subset of data outside your planning system before deciding to use it.

Organizational Issues in Demand Planning

The Demand planning function may not be defined in a fixed manner across all departments of a company. Different departments within a company and different business processes among supply chain partners, have varying requirements for Demand information. This becomes even more complex when there are multiple business entities within the company, following different business processes. Think of a company that works across a dozen countries in five different businesses with half a dozen different softwares and different planning teams and you get the picture.

Although these requirements are unique in every company, the following breakdown of needs is typical for many organizations:

Marketing

Marketing creates demand projections to determine future expected sales levels and trends in products, brands, and categories. It tends to work with medium- and long-term demand projections focusing on the market or brand level. Marketing's goal is to positively affect the projected demand to meet goals. Therefore, it is important that marketing understands the drivers of demand and the effects of modifying resource allocation to affect the demand drivers. To accomplish this task, marketing will perform detailed analysis of historical data to determine price sensitivity, media responsiveness, event effectiveness, and current and future product mix. Marketing is therefore likely to want to test potential actions through "what if" analyses and will use demand projections to:

- Determine marketing mix
- Plan new product introductions
- Identify products reaching maturity
- Build promotional calendars
- Determine prices

- Identify and determine cannibalization effects of new products and promotions
- Evaluate and monitor marketing plans, promotions, pricing etc.

Sales

Sales uses demand projections to set account level sales targets. Similar to marketing, the sales group is also responsible, at the account level, for positively affecting sales. Therefore, it too must understand the drivers of demand. Sales tend to work with short- and medium-term demand projections focusing on the account level. Sales management often asks field personnel to review and adjust forecasts based on local market knowledge. The sales organization provides input to the plan and uses the output of the plan to:

- Review accounts and adjust account-level forecasts
- Plan and execute account-specific events and promotions
- Evaluate and monitor category performance by account
- Measure projected sales versus actual plan/target by account
- Evaluate and monitor marketing plans, promotions, price actions, etc. by account.

Operations

Operations uses demand projections to drive all downstream supply chain decisions while simultaneously minimizing inventory and maintaining customer service. Operations provide the link between the demand plan and its execution by using the plan to:

- Make short-term decisions that are necessary to drive manufacturing and replenishment requests
- Manage customer inventories
- Make medium-term purchasing decisions
- Make long-term decisions, such as construction of new facilities
- Manage vendor relationships
- Drive material and plant capacity decisions

- Guide purchasing (contracts) negotiations
- Estimate transportation resource requirements

Operations work at the level of detail necessary to drive production - the stock keeping unit (SKU) level. Operations are likely to use "what if" scenarios to test capacity limitations and simulate the effects of decisions prior to execution.

Finance

Finance uses demand projections as input to set budgets, guide investor expectations, and determine cash flow. They are likely to focus on currency and are interested in aggregate figures derived from customer demand such as revenue, cost, and profit.

In all areas of the company, accuracy of forecasting and user-friendliness are common requirements. However, because each organization's focus is unique, planning requirements may vary in the following areas:

- Time horizon of forecasts
- Number of products
- Level of detail (SKU, product family, brand, etc.)
- Volume of explicative information (pricing, display penetration, advertising budgets)
- Automatic processing vs. interactive simulation
- Detailed periodicity (daily, weekly, quarterly)

Depending on the business needs of each organization — logistics, sales, marketing, and finance — the time horizon for forecasts increases correspondingly. Therefore, it becomes necessary to move from simple models based on historical sales, to more sophisticated models which are influenced by causal factors. Accordingly, both the forecast quality and the volume of the necessary information increase significantly.

Supply Chain Planning

Supply Chain uses forecast accuracy and bias as parameters and champions continuous improvement programs to improve the quality of the forecast. Supply Chain also owns the Demand Plans as well as the Supply / Fulfilment Plans and coordinates with all other teams to achieve consensus. In many companies Supply Chain will also own the coordination and conducting of the S&OP process.

Supply Chain is mainly interested in the in the following areas:

- Quality of forecasts
- Continuous improvement to Forecasting Scenarios
- Aggregate and Lower level forecasts for S&OP
- Pre-S&OP Meetings
- S&OP Meetings
- Demand Planners Day-in-life process

IT

IT owns the Demand Planning Tools, their implementations, upgrades and Rollouts. IT will also contract services of vendors for Support and Maintenance and for providing the changes required to the Demand Planning Applications as needed by the other Teams.IT would be interested in the following areas related to Demand Planning:

- Systems Integration (Ensuring systems talk to each other)
- Impact of Business Process on the Demand Planning System
- Business Intelligence and Report Generation
- User imported and maintained Data
- Backup and Archival of Demand Planning Data
- Access to, and speed of performance of Demand Planning Systems

Demand Planner FAQ's

The Demand Planner may also be called by different titles in different companies, (Demand Manager / Analyst etc.) but his is a key role in any company with a Demand side interest. There may also be Demand Teams where more than one Demand planner reports into a Demand Manager, who coordinates the total Demand Plan. Some of the frequently asked questions regarding Demand Planners are given below:

- **Which department should the Demand Planner report to?**
  The Demand Planner (Or planners) should be a cross functional role which cuts across all other department without reporting into any specific department like Sales or Marketing. Some companies think that because Sales and Marketing deal with the Demand side of the company, Demand Planning should report to them and supply planning should report into Operation. This continues to propagate the silo mentality and confrontational attitudes that a planning function should be looking to resolve. Instead the best structures that have been found to work are where the Demand Planning (and supply planning) teams report into a single supply chain or planning department, which acts as a service centre to all stakeholders ensuring a balanced point of view.

- **How many Demand Planners do you need?**
  This is a very frequent question and depends on a number of factors
  - How is your Planning team structured?
  - Will transaction systems provide most data required.
  - Will planning be done at many levels?
  - Is the Planner (planners) properly trained in systems and business process?
  - Do you have documented procedures covering all key scenarios?
  - The amounts of business exceptions you want reviewed.

- What is the total number of SKUs to be planned? How many of these are touched by the planners on an average.
- How may planned SKUs are promoted and how frequently.
- How many customers/ accounts do you have?
- What is the rate of New Product introduction?
- What is the level at which planning is done.
- How complex is your planning system.

The more automated system you have, the less Demand Planners you need. The more exceptions that you want the planners to maintain and take action on, the more Planners you need. As a rule of thumb the following can be taken as guidelines (only product dimension considered here):

- Extensive planning / Monthly S&OP and Consensus meetings / Promotions/weekly buckets - 300 to 500 SKUs per planner
- Few promotions/ No Demand consensus or collaboration/ No S&OP/weekly buckets - 700 to 1000 SKUs per planner
- DC level Planning/ weekly buckets - 1000 to 1500 SKUs per planner

	Example
Total Week Hrs	40
Planning Role	40%
Coordinating Role	40%
Other	20%
Planning Week Hrs	16
Planning Week Minutes	960

Remember that planning forecasts should only be part of his responsibilities with other time dedicated to coordination, self-learning, innovations etc. As an example, out of a total of 40 Hrs. per week the planner is probably left with 960 minutes after accounting for other activities ,so even if he plans 1 SKU a minute (very unrealistic) he can only own a maximum of 960 SKUs. The trick is to automate your Demand Planning system so that the planner works by exception and does not have to work / look at all SKUs in every planning cycle.

In any case a company should have a second line of planners/ shadow planners to assist the key planners and take on the role in case of leave / vacations etc. One of the easiest ways for losing Demand Planning capabilities is to simply lose your Key Demand Planner to another competitor, or to have them move into another role. Shadow Planners may have part responsibilities or may have other main roles and ensure that your Demand Planners are not overloaded during peak season or promotional periods.

- **Do the Demand Planners need to be aware of supply Plans?**
  The Demand Planner needs to be aware of supply side constraints and any modifications to the supply plans if they have an impact on short term or long term Demand Plans. Any adjustments to forecasts for this are however best done in the S&OP sessions. For example it wouldn't make sense forecasting and generating a Demand Plan for a SKU if Supply cannot manufacture or source the product or any government regulation affects the supply of the product adversely. This can especially be valid for products that are imported or sourced or have long lead times.

- **Should you have a common Demand and Supply Planner?**
  Some companies have a common Demand and Supply function handled by the same Planner. This can be applicable for companies which have very limited number of SKUs or in Make to order scenarios where products are manufactured/ sourced against advance customer orders.
  The usual practice is to have separate Demand Planners and Supply Planners. Or just have Demand Planners in case there is no manufacturing or sourcing function.

- **Does the Demand Planner have a Business, Forecasting or a systems role?**
  The Demand Planner should primarily be a business role but he needs to have an understanding of basic statistics, modelling, forecasting and operating your Demand Planning System. Other skills needed would be good coordination and stakeholder management, communication and presentation.

Thought Points........

- [ ] Who should the Demand Planner report to.
How would the Demand Planners Day-in-Life be impacted
If a company had daily planning cycles and time buckets.

- [ ] Why does a Demand Planner need to attend the S&OP Meetings.
What does a Demand Planner do with the output from S&OP Meetings.

- [ ] What should a planner do when he encounters issues.
Should the Demand Planner be worried about supply side issues.

- [ ] Who owns the Promotional Uplift Forecast.
What can the Demand Planner do if there is no historical data for a product.

notes.................

notes....................

notes..................

Chapter 4

Managing History

One of the first things that an organization has to determine is, 'what should be considered as History'? There are multiple options available to every company. Some of these are given below:

- Historical POS sales Data.
- Shipments from DCs to Stores.
- Orders placed by Stores onto DCs.
- Customer Order History.
- Historical customer order data.
- Historical shipments from a Manufacturing plant to a DC.

> **Note:** Definition of History Data should be a one-time activity done at the time of designing or implementing a Demand Planning solution.

There are two common options used by companies: Sales History (at different levels) or Shipment History from a DC or a Manufacturer.

Store Level Sales History

The history in this case is sales from each Store (in a retail scenario). This could be all sales aggregated to a day or week for each store.

- May be used to supplement aggregate level History
- May not be robust for modelling Trend and Seasonality
- Low Volume, High Volatility, Patchy Data
- High Number of SKUs
- High number of Planners needed
- Most statistical algorithms won't be much better than simple averages.
- User input and additional factors needed to improve accuracy.

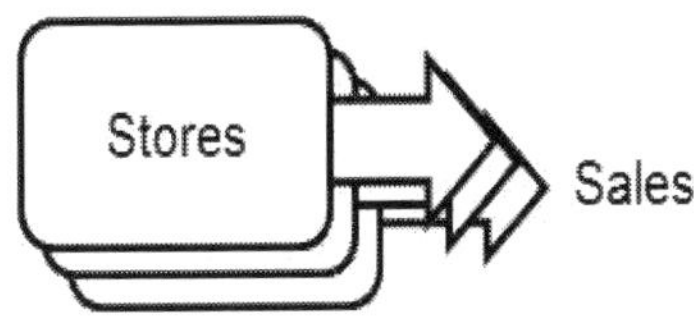

Aggregated Store Level Sales History

The history in this case is aggregated sales for all stores by SKU from each Store (in a retail scenario).

- Robust history for modelling Trend and Seasonality
- Manageable Number of SKUs
- Small number of Planners needed
- Most statistical algorithms can be applied to generate good forecast.
- Demand Plan can be useful for aggregate planning but not for store level planning.

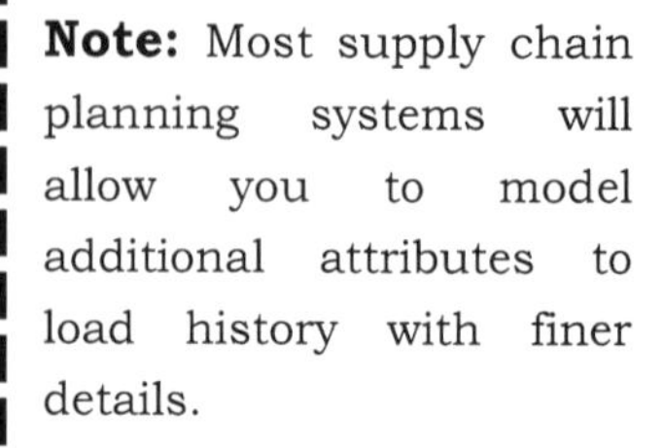
Note: Most supply chain planning systems will allow you to model additional attributes to load history with finer details.

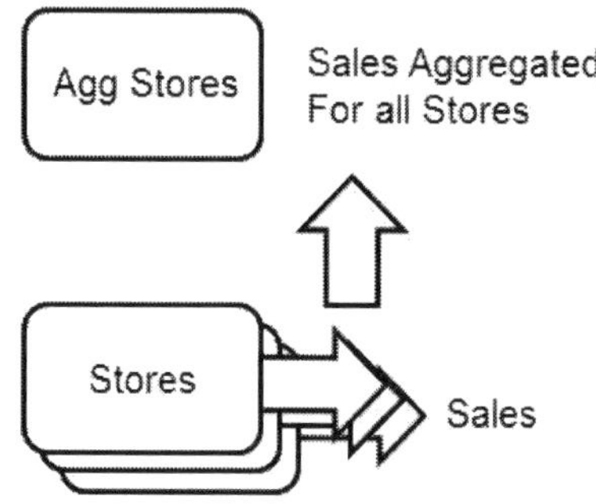

DC to Stores Shipment History

The history in this case is shipments from a DC aggregated for all stores. i.e. total SKU quantity shipped out of a DC irrespective of its destination.

- Does not reflect true demand
- May hide the true trend and Seasonality of Demand
- Shipment History would be effected by supply and other constraints
- Easier to model as the data is at a aggregation
- High Volume, Low Volatility
- Low Number of SKUs
- Low number of Planners needed

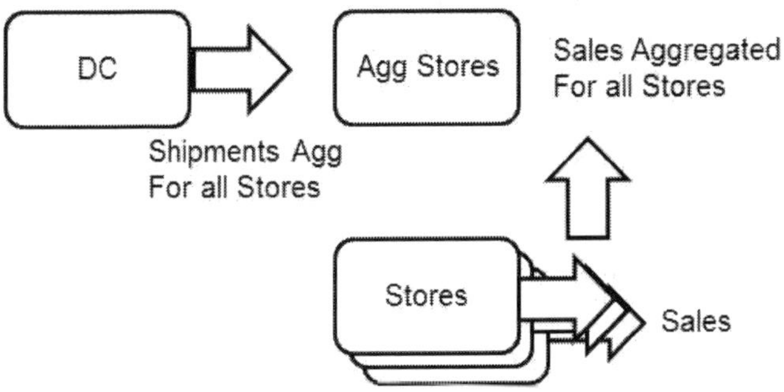

Manufacturers Outbound Shipment History

The history in this case is aggregated shipments outbound from a Manufacturer (either to a DC, a Customer Account or Retailer).

- History reflects customer/retailer ordering patterns as well as supply constraints of Manufacturer.
- The real customer demand is not visible.
- Easier to model as the data is at a aggregation
- High Volume, High Volatility
- Low Number of SKUs
- High number of Planners needed to incorporate constant changes

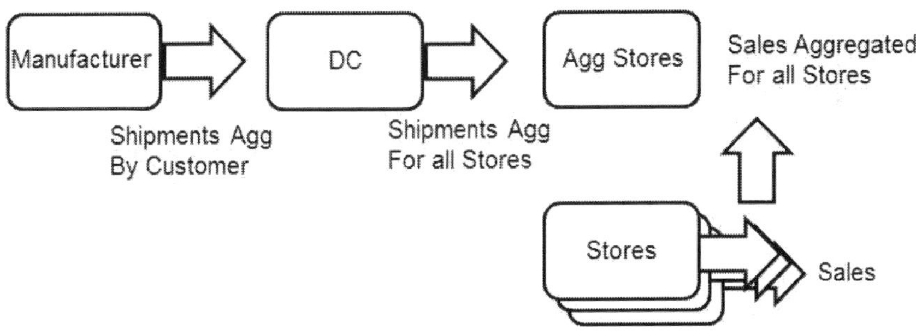

History Decomposition

In most cases the history that is loaded into your demand planning systems will consist of replicating seasonal patterns as well as non-replicating patterns that may have occurred due to internal or external events. In case of Internal Events (like promotions, markdowns, new product launch, supplier push, trade promotions and volume discounts etc.) the company may have additional historical information to explain the irregular patterns. In case of External Events (like natural disasters, freak weather, one off sports events like Olympics etc) there may or may not be historical data to explain the irregular patterns. These irregular patterns can be unnatural peaks, dips or zero history periods. History Decomposition is the process of identifying and separating these non-repeating patterns from the Raw History to arrive at a Base History, representing demand patterns that would have occurred without the impact of any internal or external factors. This Base History is then used as the input for generating the statistical forecast for normal sales. This statistical forecast would represent only the expected sales for normal demand and would then be enriched with impact of future promotions, external events and strategic management targets.

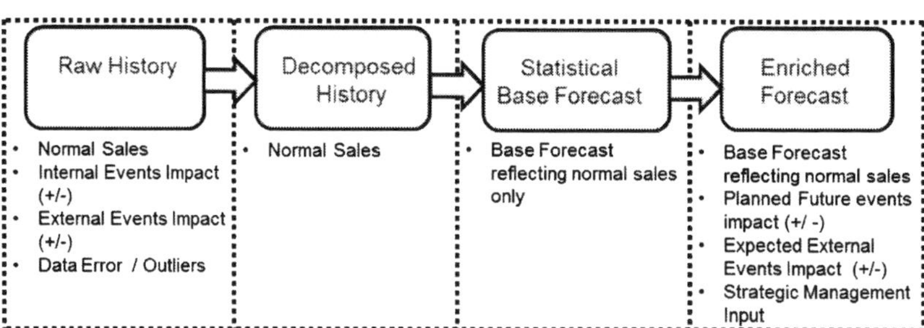

History Decomposition is most beneficial for companies actively driving and modelling their demand with promotions, innovation and strategic direction. A key point to note is that this is of use only for SKUs where you have robust and reasonable amount of history.

History Decomposition should be the first step at the beginning if every planning cycle, before a forecast is generated. The most common options used to Decompose History are:

- **Manual**: In this case the planner manually edits, modifies or excludes history points after history is loaded into the Demand Planning System. This can become a cumbersome process that needs to be repeated regularly as new history is added. This also brings in the human judgement and associated errors and should usually only be performed on an exception basis. Most Demand Planning systems will maintain a record of the original history and the change made by the planner in case the manual correction needs to be reversed. This approach may be taken in case there are very few SKUs, or the SKUs have very robust history with minimal need for Decomposition. An initial evaluation of history may be done outside the system to decide if this is the case, and to evaluate if the resultant workload would be manageable. Some Demand Planning systems allow enhanced functionality to support manual editing. This may range from editing multiple periods at the same time, rule based editing, selective exclusion of history points, to applying the same edits to multiple SKUs.

- **Automatic-Causal Factor Based**: In this case historical information related to events in the past is available to the company and is used by the Demand Planning system to identify periods where the historical demand was impacted by an event. These could be internal events like promotions or external events like strike by transporters. This however means that additional data needs to be imported and maintained in the system. Additionally the factors may not fully explain the extent of the impact. In most Demand Planning systems the forecasting algorithms will usually compute the strength and impact of the historical factors automatically and then remove them from History.

- **Automatic Threshold Parameters based**: Some of the advanced Demand Planning systems allow the Demand Planner to set upper and lower thresholds for History outliers. Any value that is not a seasonal pattern and lies above the upper threshold, or below the lower threshold from the mean, are then identified. The threshold values are usually set at aggregate levels (country / brand etc.) to reduce maintenance and workload for planners.

  The Threshold values are usually applied as one of the below:

  - **Standard Deviation values from mean.** This defines the spread zone above and below the mean of a SKU where decomposed history values are expected to be found.
  - **%age values from mean.** This defines the percentage range above and below the mean of a SKU where decomposed history values are expected to be found.
  - **Absolute value limits.** This defines an absolute upper or lower limit over (or under) which the history values should not be expected to be present.

  Any values found outside the threshold values are then treated in one of three ways (discussed in more detail later in this chapter):

  - Values adjusted to upper and lower thresholds.
  - Values adjusted to average history.
  - Values ignored or set to zero.

Often a company will use a mix of all three of the above approaches with manual changes made on an exception bases before the automatic decomposition has been done. The automated component of History Decomposition may not always be visible as a separate process, and some Demand Planning systems incorporate this as an internal process of the Forecasting Algorithm.

An example of the steps taken to decompose History is given below. This is a generic description at a high level and in some cases the sequence of the steps may be different. For example any manual editing of history may be done after the automatic processes.

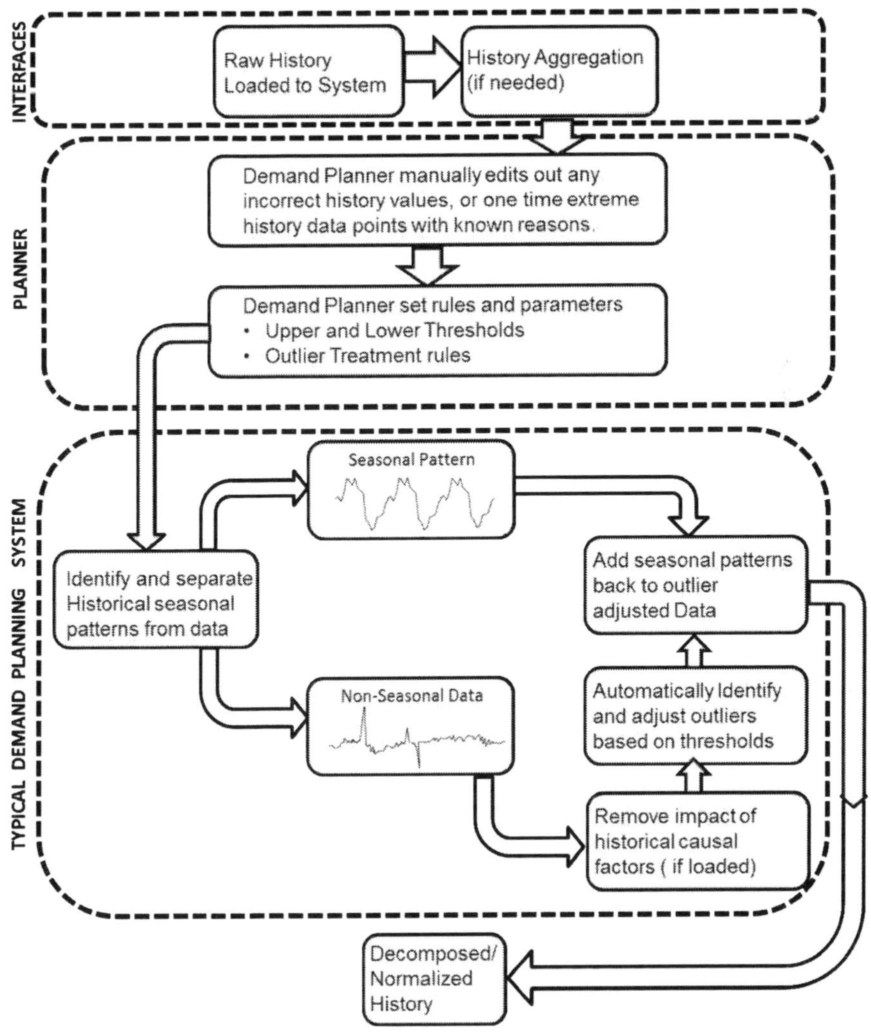

Historical Causal Factors

Often a company may decide to use more than one history data stream to compare and validate the results. The second history stream in these cases is usually for validation purpose and only one main history is used for demand planning purposes.

In certain cases companies may also decide to take into consideration additional (non-demand) History of factors that are expected to have an impact on their demand. For example:

- **Historical Prices**: This is usually important if price is expected to have an impact on demand. In case prices have changed during the history periods, a products historical demand could have had an upwards or downwards impact. It's important to take this into account while modelling your history setup. It needs to be noted that this is only important for History at individual SKU level and not at aggregate levels (as the price changes usually happen at SKU level).

- **Historical Stockout periods**: These are used if the company maintains a historical record of periods when an item has been stocked out. This is usually captured as a Yes/No option at a SKU/Location level, with the idea that the history is not correctly reflected or may need adjustment during the stockout periods.

- **Historical Order losses**: These are Historical Orders with known quantities that have not been serviced. Unlike Stockout Periods where the lost demand is not known, the company in this case knows the exact amount lost/ unsatisfied and may decide to add that back to reflect realistic demand. It should be noted that this would be applicable only in some industries/companies where advanced orders are placed by customers. Also an unsatisfied demand should then, not have been satisfied in the next period otherwise there would be a complex history adjustment exercise that would need to be followed.

- **Temperature:** Historical Temperature is sometimes used as an additional factor by companies who have product demand affected by temperature and weather. An ice cream or beer company may have its demand affected by increasing temperatures or sudden spikes in temperature in a country. In such cases the temperature can be modelled as a causal factor impacting the demand of products.

> **Note:** One key point related to multiple history data streams is to select only the ones that have a visible and measurable impact and where history has been maintained for a reasonably long period of time.
> Your Demand Planning systems should also be flexible enough to handle the additional History data streams.

- **Number of stores**: This is applicable in a retail scenario where a company is increasing (or decreasing) its total number of stores and the History is at an aggregated store or DC level. In such cases if the number of stores increases, the total history is no longer representative of the total demand for the future and needs to be adjusted by the total number of stores.

- **Number of products**: This may be used by an organization in case they use aggregated SKU level History (e.g. for Raw Material forecasting).In such cases using an additional data stream of number of SKUs could be used to model historical and future demand.

- **Historical promotion periods**: This is used by companies to identify historical periods where a product was promoted to adjust and treat the history for those periods differently.

- **Historical Marketing and Advertising**: Historical periods when a product or group of products, or a brand has been promoted are expected to have an impact of the Marketing on their demand. It is possible to use an additional data stream to identify these periods and adjust the history for their estimated impact.

History FAQ's

The Demand Planner needs to be aware of the following decisions / configurations made within your Demand Planning solution and the reasons for the decisions. Some of these may impact regular planning cycle while others may be a one-time decision at the time of implementing your Demand Planning solution. In any case these should be reviewed at least once every year. There may also be need for ad hoc changes required in case of major issues with History.

- **What History Timebuckets will be used?** Will History be loaded in Daily, Weekly or Monthly TimeBuckets? Some Advanced Demand Planning solutions allow you to Load History in smaller timebuckets and automatically aggregate them to higher buckets if required. A forecast generated out of a History will have the same timebuckets as the History used to generate it.

- **What History Loading Frequency will be followed?** Will the history be loaded for a week every week or two weeks every week (or any other frequency). For example a retailer working with aggregated sales for all stores as history may want to load two weeks of History as some of their stores may not have reported the full sales by the cutoff date within the week. Or they may simply not be connected with real time data.

- **When will the History be loaded?** How are your weekly (or monthly) buckets defined and what day of the week will you load the History into your Demand Planning solution. For example a company could define its Demand Planning week as Mon to Sunday and aggregate all sales from Monday to Sunday and Load it in you Demand Planning solution on Sunday Evening. As this will drive the new Demand Planning cycle it needs to be decided in coordination with other planning teams as there is a dependency on its supply side planning cycle as well as other systems processing schedule.

- **How much History is needed to accurately model Demand?** The optimum number of History required to model at the SKU Level is two years history. Some companies maintain 3 years History if their products have long lead times, or if they want to maintain the extra history for validations , reporting and data mining purposes (for example historical promotions)
  The two years history is enough to capture any replicating seasonality or Demand Patterns. Any shorter History would mean that complete seasonality patterns may not be captured. Seasonality by definition is annual patterns that repeat, and can only be verified once they happen twice. Very short History SKUs may have to be excluded from statistical planning and managed manually due to lack of data. Longer Histories than 3 years can cause performance issues with the Demand Planning system and slow it down as the additional data is processed. Additionally in most industries the long gone past probably is not representative and may not act as a good indicator of future demand. More intelligent Demand Planning Systems will allow you to define a start date from which a History will be considered for planning/ modelling purposes.

- **How much History is loaded on a regular basis?** After the one of initial load of History when your Demand Planning Solution is setup for the first time, you will usually have only small updates of history being added for the most recent time periods. Given below are some options of loading History when planning in weekly timebuckets (the weeks can be replaced by months in case of monthly buckets.):

  a) Load History for every incremental week as the week finishes.

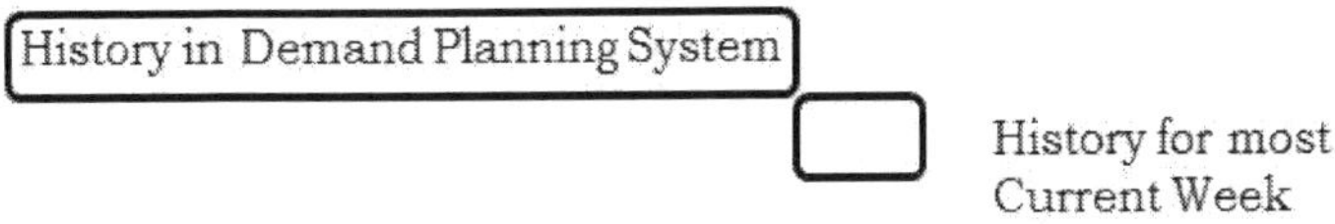

History in Demand Planning System

History for most Current Week

b) Load History for the last two most current weeks as the current week finishes. This can be done when you are not very confident of most recent history and want it updated on a regular basis.

History in Demand Planning System

History for most Current 2 Weeks

c) Load History on a daily basis as each day finishes and aggregate the daily history to a weekly timebucket when the week is complete.

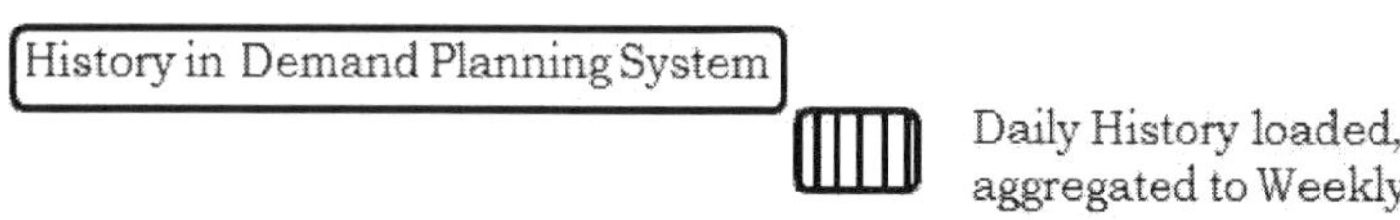

- **Do we consider all History as equal**? There may be cases where older history is no longer representative of a SKUs demand as the product may have declined in sales (or increased its average sales level). In such cases it's beneficial if we can place an increased weightage on the most recent history while modelling the SKU. Many Demand Planning systems will allow the Planner to define weightage parameters or discount factors to place more weightage on recent history and then automatically apply the impact.

- **At what level should the History be loaded?** Firstly, History should be loaded at only one level within your Demand Planning System. This ensures that there is a single source of History even if you aggregate History or forecast to higher levels within your system. It also ensures consistency in History at different levels. Secondly History should be loaded at the lowest level that the forecast would be required by any of the organization team members. Loading any lower or granular level History will only slow the system down with unnecessary data and increase workload.

- **How is the History maintained/deleted**? As the timeline moves forward, History will continue to grow within your Demand Planning System. This can slow down your Demand Planning System and also lead to incorrect models if very old history gets included. Demand Planning systems will not automatically delete extra history and most companies have to delete it from their systems using customised code or manually. Two practices widely used are:

    a) Annual deletion of History over two (or three) years every yes (e.g. every January). This ensures seasonality is correctly maintained, but has the disadvantage of a large chunk of data getting removed suddenly which can cause visible changes to trends etc. This can of course me managed by doing it on a test system or smaller dataset and observing the impact.

    b) Rolling deletion of History (either monthly or quarterly). This ensures that only smaller chunks of data are removed and the history is constantly maintained at two years in your Demand Planning system, with history over two years (or three years) regularly being deleted. This option may however result in incorrect seasonality patters being reflected.

- **What happens to the deleted Historical data?** Most companies do not permanently delete the history but just remove the History from your demand planning system. This is either stored offline in databases or in archival systems. It should also be noted that usually other related data will be deleted and archived along with History. There is no point in maintaining data related to promotions, prices etc. if the history is removed.

- **What is the source system for History?** Is this system going to be changed or replaced in the future? Most of the time the History data in automatically imported into your Demand Planning System from your Transaction / ERP systems. In any case there should be a single and stable source of History. Of course different History streams may be loaded from different sources. For example History quantity in could be loaded from your ERP system and prices History loaded from a separate Financial system. The planner needs to be aware of the sources of these data and be involved in case any of the source systems are being replaced, upgraded or face issues.

- **What is the unit of History?** History in most cases is loaded in Unit quantities but the Unit quantities themselves could be single units, cases, pallets, truckloads, tonnes etc. This is a key decision which should be made at the time your Demand Planning System is implemented and the Demand Planner should understand the background and rationale. There are even companies who might find it useful to load History in financial numbers. Most advanced Demand Planning Systems now allow the planner to convert the units internally within the system using conversion factors, but these can be cumbersome and inflexible.

- **Is there any exclusion that needs to be made before History is loaded?** In some cases there may be data that makes sense to be excluded from history for Demand Planning purposes. Some examples are, returns from customers causing negative history, History in decimals or under a specific minimum values etc.

- **Is there any pre-processing of History needed before History is loaded?** In some cases there may be a validation or processing of history done before it is loaded into your Demand Planning systems. Some examples are : converting decimals to zeroes, adjusting negative history, converting History to different units, setting history under a specified value to zero etc.

Historical Outliers

A History outlier is an extreme historical value that can Skew the mean, create false patterns and generally cause havoc for a SKUs forecast. An outlier usually has the following characteristics:

- An Outlier has to be an exception and an infrequent value. A SKU that is very volatile and has frequent peaks and troughs cannot have all the peaks identified as Outliers.
- An outlier is usually identified when you have a long and stable history broken by some exceptionally high values.
- An outlier cannot be identified for new products or products with very short history.
- Outliers need to be distinct from seasonality patterns, which basically mean that they are expected to be non-repeating patterns.

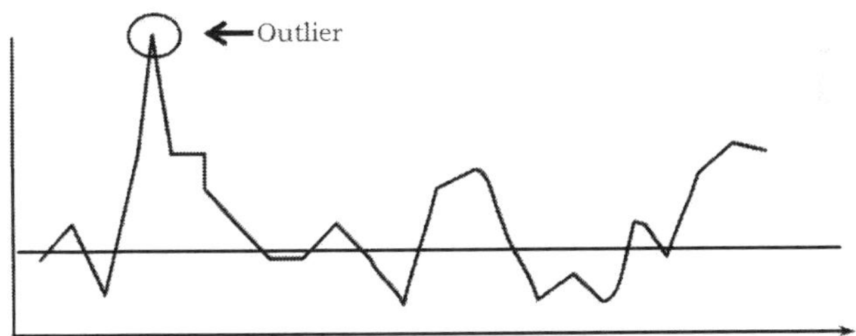

The Impact of Outliers

The reason History outliers are considered undesirable is that even a single extreme value can adversely impact the Forecasting model of a SKU. Consider the very simplistic data below: A SKU sells 10 units every day for 10 weeks giving us a mean value of 10 for the SKU.

Wk1	Wk2	Wk3	Wk4	Wk5	Wk6	Wk7	Wk8	Wk9	Wk10	Sum	Mean
10	10	10	10	10	10	10	10	10	10	100	10

Next we consider the same data but with a single outlier value of 110 for week 1. We can clearly see that there is a jump in the mean for the SKU by 100% because of the single outlier value, from 10 to 20. This is of course not desirable as the mean for the whole forecasted period could be increased incorrectly.

Wk1	Wk2	Wk3	Wk4	Wk5	Wk6	Wk7	Wk8	Wk9	Wk10	Sum	Mean
110	10	10	10	10	10	10	10	10	10	200	20

Options to address Outliers

Most Demand Planning Systems in the market will offer one or more ways to identify and address Outliers in History to remove their impact. Outliers are mostly identified based on threshold parameters in relation to the mean of all the History Data for a SKU. There are some Systems that offer more intelligent ways of identifying outliers based on whether they fit the expected pattern and model of a SKUs History or not. Given below are a few ways these systems can handle the outliers:

- Ignore the Outlier – The Outlier value can be excluded from calculations. This may however, damp the overall pattern if you have more than one or two outliers in two years of History. It also assumes your Demand Planning system has the capability to exclude the outlier from all calculations instead of just considering the History Value as zero for that period.
- Set the Outlier Value to the mean of all other values- This replaces the Outlier with the mean value for the SKU and ensures the History period has no positive and negative impact.
- Set the Outlier Value to the maximum of all other values- This replaces the Outlier with the next maximum value (or a specified upper threshold) for the SKU. There is however, a risk that this value itself may be identified as an Outlier.
- Set the Outlier value to a user specified value- In this case the Planner edits or sets the value of the Outlier to a manually set value. This can be done in case the Planner recognizes the outlier and its cause and is in a position to suggest an alternate value.

Thought Points........

- ☐ Can you load History in Monthly Buckets and generate forecast in weekly buckets in your Demand Planning System. Can you load History at a aggregate SKU/National Level and generate forecast at a granular SKU/Store Level.
- ☐ How much history of a causal factor do you need for a SKU. What can you do if you have data for multiple causal factors available for a SKU.
- ☐ What could happen if you don't delete History regularly. Is it advisable to reload all history data for a SKU everytime history is loaded each week.
- ☐ What would happen if Outliers are not identified and corrected in History. Can you identify Outliers for a SKU with one year of History.

notes.............

notes..................

notes..............

Chapter 5

Key Forecasting Concepts

Forecasting is the first step towards planning. Planning by its nature is done for the future and in case of a company, it starts with an estimate of the Future Demand. The Forecasting process is aimed at reducing the uncertainty around the future by using history as an indicator and by using as much other information as possible within the limited time available for planning.

Many factors influence the Future Demand for a product. These factors can be internal or external to the company. Forecasting is usually done based on the internal data available within a company, sometimes supported by external factors if they are expected to have a significant impact on the Demand of a product. So while it may be ok to generate a forecast for a can of beans based on internal company data (History, Promotions etc.), another company that sells ice cream or beer may decide to take into account external data as well in their forecast models (Temperature, Weather Forecasts etc.). Demand is also affected by artificial patterns like days of the week, salary payment cycles , month-ends , financial year ends etc. some of these patterns may be regular while others may vary from period to period. Add to this the fact that all forecasts have an element of error and you will start to get a glimpse of the complexity of the Forecasting process. However, Forecasting itself is a smaller sub-process with the Demand Planning Function.

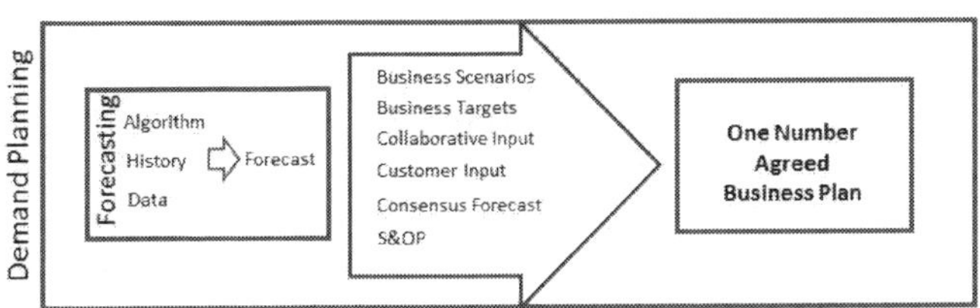

Features Common to All Forecasts

A wide variety of forecasting techniques are in use. In many respects they are quite different from each other, however all of them have some common features:

- **Causality**: Forecasting techniques generally assume that the conditions and drivers of demand that existed in the past will continue to exist in the future and will drive the same customer behaviour and demand.

- **Error**: All Forecasts have errors and actual results are expected to differ from predicted values. The value of the Forecasting function lies in constantly trying to minimize this error and to improve the confidence of the business in their planning numbers.

- **Bias**: All Forecasts are biased. This can be due to Data, Human Bias, System Bias, Algorithms, and Trend Projections. A Forecast Bias is an intentional or unintentional influence on the Statistical Forecast, which could in some cases be undesirable. A consistent positive or negative bias to the forecast could result in extra inventory in the supply chain or stockouts.

- **Law of Big Numbers**: Aggregate level Forecasts or Forecasts for groups of items are usually more accurate than Granular Forecasts (or Forecasts for individual SKUs) because forecasting errors among SKUs in a group usually have a cancelling effect at an aggregate level.

- **Law of Time Horizon**: Forecast accuracy usually decreases as the Forecasting Time Horizon increases. This is closely linked to supply Lead Times and when the forecast is actually generated. A short Horizon forecast generated at the last minute could be highly inaccurate if the company doesn't have time to respond and fulfil the demand.

Elements of a Good Forecast

- **The Forecast should be available in time.** Usually, a certain amount of time is needed to respond to the information contained in a forecast. For example, capacity cannot be expanded overnight, nor can inventory levels be changed immediately. Hence, the forecasting horizon must cover the time necessary to take action.

- **The Forecast should be as accurate as possible** within the data conditions. Accuracy should be measured and recorded. This will enable users to plan for possible errors and will provide a basis for comparing alternative forecasts.

- **The Forecast should be consistent and explainable.** An algorithm that randomly provides a good forecast or a poor forecast without any justification will only cause a lack of confidence in the forecasts and the forecasting process.

- **The Forecast should be expressed in useful units** for the Business. The CFO could need it converted to financial units, the Operations Team in pallets or manufacturing lots and the DCs by space.

- **The Forecast should be recorded and measured.** Forecasting is a journey of improvement and you cannot improve what you do not measure. This also helps direct the planners and the business focus on where most value can be added.

- **The Forecasting Algorithm should be simple to operate.** It doesn't help if you need great statisticians to operate or understand your forecasting algorithm and process. Within an organization you will find people leaving and new people joining, and it helps if your forecasting technique is simple to understand and operate.

Defining a Forecasting Process

The high level basic steps in defining a forecasting process are given below. Note that this is not something that the Demand Planner would do regularly as the first five points are usually a one off activity while the rest are iterative. This also does not cover the wider Demand Planning steps:

- **Decide what needs to be Forecasted**. Are you forecasting sales from stores or shipments from DCs? Is it finished goods, or components and Raw Material as well?
- **Define the Consumer of the Forecast**. Who is going to use the Forecast, is it operations for manufacturing, buying to send to suppliers, the CFO for strategic planning.. or all of them!
- **Define the Usage of the Forecast**. What is its purpose and when will it be needed? This will provide an indication of the level of detail required in the forecast, the amount of resources needed, and the level of accuracy necessary.
- **Establish the Forecast Characteristics**. Its time horizon, level of forecasting, Forecasting Time Buckets and Forecasting Units.
- **Select a Forecasting System**. This needs to have a good fit in handling the points above.
- **Gather and segment data**. Before a forecast can be prepared, data must be gathered, analysed and segmented. This is done to determine planning techniques, algorithms and parameters.
- **Generate the Statistical forecast**. The system would use the selected algorithm in generating a Statistical Forecast. The emphasis here is on “Statistical”, as the final forecast after other planner inputs could be very different.
- **Monitor the forecast**. The statistical forecast needs to be reasonably accurate and good before any of the other intelligence can be added. To achieve this, it’s key that the Statistical Forecast be monitored to determine whether it is performing in a satisfactory manner.

Forecasting Models

A Forecasting Model is a set of rules and assumptions that are used to work on a set of data, to provide future forecasts. Forecasting Models and usually placed in three groups for ease of understanding:

Naïve Forecasts: These are models that generate forecasts using the most basic rules. In these Models all the Forecasting rules are pre-specified and no parameter values need to be applied by the Planner.

Statistical Forecasts: These are models that generate forecasts using statistical rules and models applied to historical data. These are mainly Time Series Models (called Time Series as they work on Historical data across a series of Time buckets).

Judgemental Forecasts: These are models that apply manual inputs or intelligence based on peoples experience and expertise. These reflect expectations that may or may not have historical data to support the forecasts. The input is market knowledge and sometimes even intuition and ideas about what is likely to happen in the future.

In actual practice, Time-Series Models and Judgmental Models are rarely used on their own. Most companies will use a combination of Time Series as well as Judgemental inputs to arrive at a usable Forecast. Planners may run a Time-Series Based Model but change a few figures, applying their intelligence (judgment) to periods for which they think quantities may be different. In many cases the Forecasting Model selection is driven by the following factors.

- The amount and quality of data available.
- The number of planners and other resources available.
- The capability of your current/ future software.
- The overall Demand Planning process/ framework.

Main Types of Forecasting Models

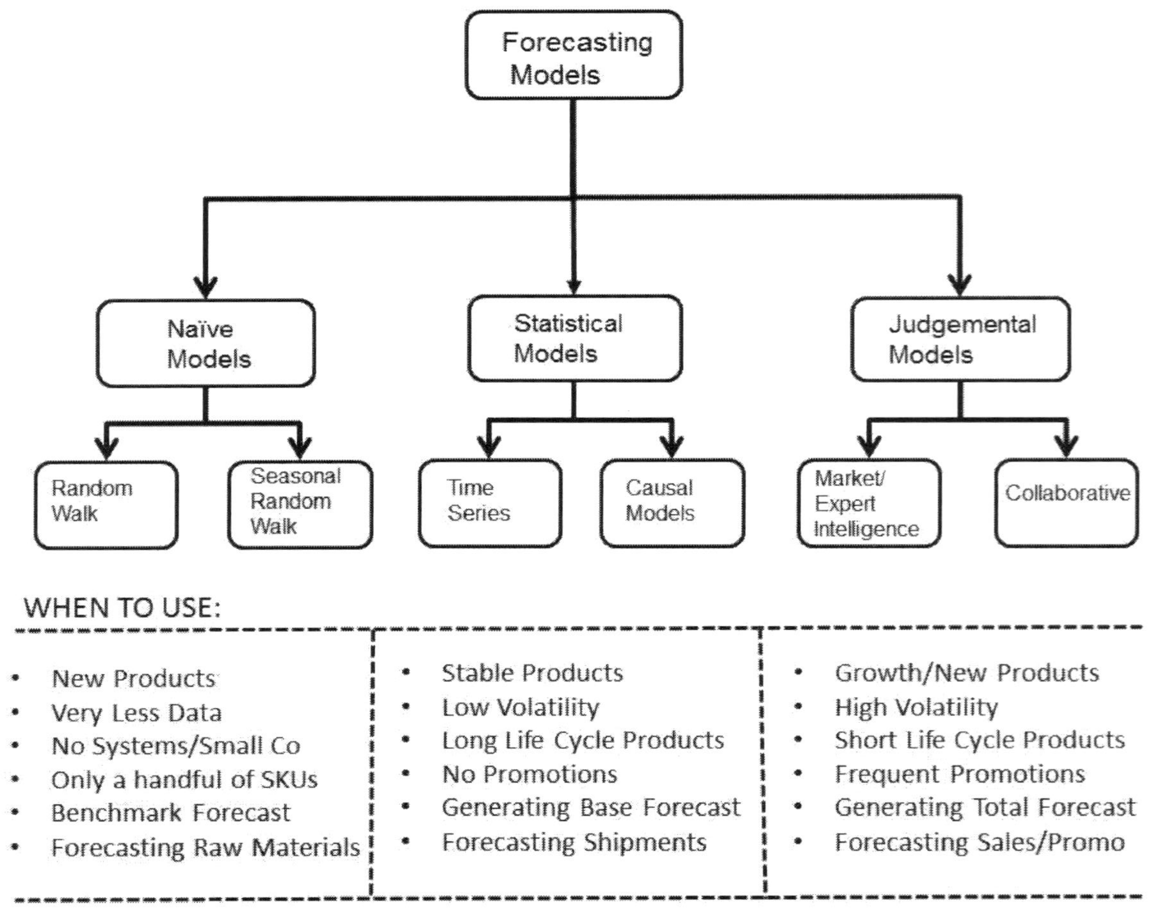

Naïve Forecasts

Naïve forecasting models are based on historical observation and use simple models to project future demand. These models do not attempt to explain the underlying relationship between the historical observations and the forecasts generated. There are no explanations of the historical patterns (for example Trends, seasonality etc) and no additional data inputs required from the planners.

Naive models may be classified into two groups. One group consists of simple projection models. These models require inputs of data from recent observations, but no statistical analysis is performed. The second group is comprised of models that, while naive, are complex enough to require a computer.

Naïve forecasts may be used:

- For generating forecasts for low volume, non critical products.
- For generating a benchmark to compare Forecast Accuracy.
- For generating Forecasts for seasonal products.

Naïve forecasts are:

- Limited in their accuracy
- Static models reapplied every time a forecast is generated

But.

- Easier to model
- Don't need sophisticated tools
- Don't need planner interventions
- In special cases perform as good as any other forecast.
- Can be used for exceptional skus which don't fit other models.

The most common approaches to Naïve forecasts are described below:

Last Historical Value as Forecast: This is the simplest of the Naïve Forecasting approaches and uses a single historical value as the basis for future forecasts.

- **Random Walk**: In this approach the most current history value is assumed as the Forecast for all future periods. The Forecast is updated as soon as new History comes in.

- **Seasonal Random Walk**: Rolling Averages: A rolling average is taken for a rolling number of historical periods and then used as Forecast for all forecasted periods.

These approaches are easily affected by fluctuations in historical data but you could use simple rules to control some of these fluctuations. For Example- updating the forecast only when the latest history value is greater than the forecast.

Averaging Models: This approach expands the historical time period over which actual history is considered, instead of just taking the most current History. This leads to a smoothing of any peaks and troughs and generates a more smoothed forecast.

- **Simple Averages**: A static average is calculated for all historical periods and used as a flat line Forecast for all future periods.

- **Moving Averages:** A rolling average is taken for a rolling number of historical periods and then used as Forecast for forecasted periods.

- **Weighted Averages:** A weighted average involves giving different weight to different historical periods while computing a moving average. For example placing a higher weight to most recent history will ensure the Forecast reflects the most recent past.

Statistical Models - Time Series

There are 3 main components to a Time Series Statistical Forecast. The Mean, the Trend and Seasonality. A fourth component is long term business cycle, but its not usually modelled within forecasting models as its time horizon is much longer than the forecasting and demand planning horizons for most businesses.

Level – The mean or the level is the average of all historical values and dictates the average level of the forecast. The Level is usually a straight line that passes through all the observed historical values. While computing the mean negative historical values are usually ignored. In some forecasting methods a Dynamic Mean may be used, which is a rolling mean generated for each historical period, using all historical values before the calculated period.

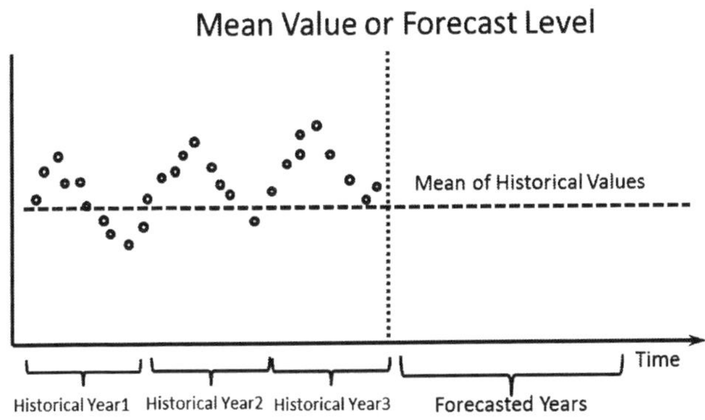

Trend – The Trend component of a forecast can be a positive or negative movement of the historical data. This is used by the forecasting models and projected into the forecasted periods if the trend is expected to continue. Some advanced Demand Planning systems use forecasting algorithms which allow you to damp the trend growth or model a decline for forecasted periods. User ability to manually define the trend is also a common functionality, but should be used in exceptional cases only, as it will override the natural trend captured from the historical data. Another useful functionality provided by some systems is the ability to define multiple trend components. A planner can then define a short term trend and a long term trend which allows him more control over the forecast. For example, a planner could model a short term upward trend, followed by a downward trend and vice versa.

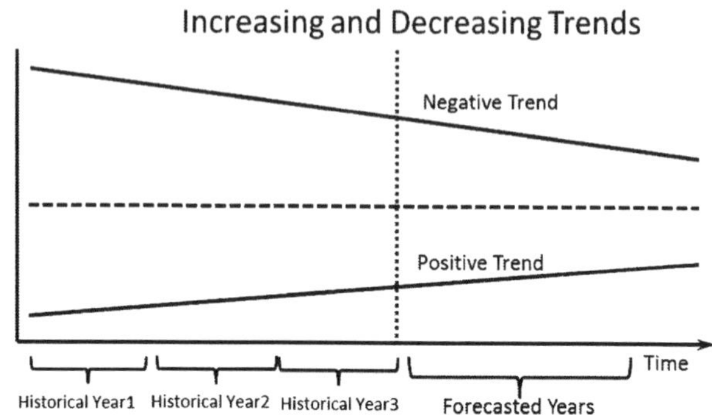

Seasonality – The seasonal component of a forecast is the projection of the pattern of seasonal peaks and troughs that can be found in the historical data. A seasonal pattern is defined as an annual recurring pattern which can be seen in the data year after year. Of course, this means that we need to have at least two years of history data to identify seasonal patterns that have occurred over at least two years. Most advanced Demand Planning systems will allow the planner to switch off the seasonality component for products with shorter history. In some applications , the planner may also have the capability to provide external seasonal patters or profiles, which would override any seasonal patterns identified by the demand planning systems within the SKUs own historical data.

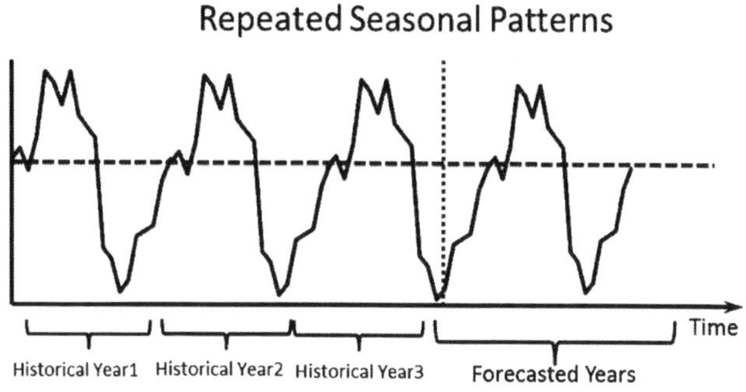

Noise – Any unexplained or residual quantities left after accounting for the Mean , Trend and Seasonality are quantified as Noise or unexplained quantities within the historical values. These values cannot be assumed to be an error that doesn't fit the forecasting model, as they have already happened. A better way of modelling and accounting for these values is to identify reasons for these values. The reasons may be internal (Promotions, price discounts , new product launch etc) or external (weather ,external events like the Olympics etc) In any case its not beneficial to have Noise within the forecasting model and the best approach is to remove then using manual input or causal factor modelling, using additional factors to explain the Noise. If the Noise cannot be explained it is filtered off in extreme cases as an outlier. The less the Noise in a forecasting model, the better the model fits to History and the better is the forecast accuracy expected from the model.

The three components are then usually combined into a forecasting model using one of the many forecasting algorithms to generate a forecast.

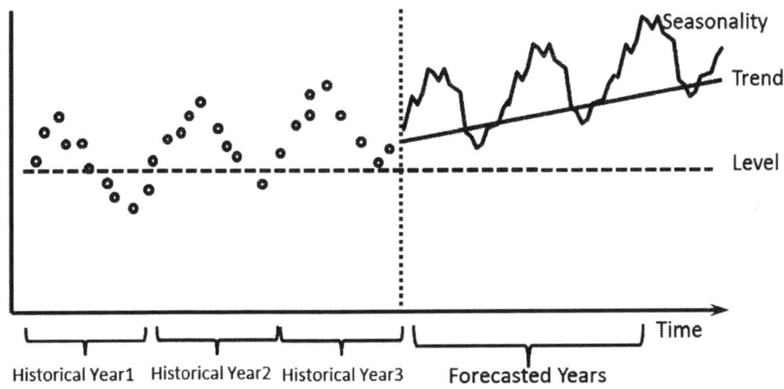

There are many Forecasting Algorithms that use the concept above in different combinations and most advanced planning systems will have more than one option available to the planner.

Statistical Models – Causal Models

In a classic Time Series Forecast we usually have one data stream being used. For example Historical Sales used to generate sales Forecast. In the Causal Models, there are one or more set of additional data streams which are expected to have an impact or "Causal relationship" on the main data stream being forecasted. For example Historical Temperature being used alongside Historical sales of Ice Creams to identify what is the impact of temperature on the sales. This Causal relationship can then be applied to future forecast to model the impact of future temperature changes.

Causal Factors – Any data which is expected to have a strong impact on the Forecast is called a Causal Factor. It's possible to have more than one such Factor to be applied in a Causal Model. However the larger the number of Factors, the more complex the model gets.

Applying Causal Models – The key steps in generating forecast using Causal Models are given below:

- **Define criteria** for a Causal Factor: Here we would define a Causal Factor based on criteria like, availability of data, applicability to your industry and business, reliability of future causal factor data etc.
- **Analysis to measure Strength** of Impact: once a short list of Factors is available, we measure the strength of impact observed across historical data.
- **Selection of Causal Factors** to be applied: The final causal factors to be applied are then selected based on the factors that have the strongest measureable impact.
- **Collection of Data** : Historical and Future Causal Factor data is then collected and loaded on a regular basis into the planning systems
- **Generation of Forecast** Using Causal Models: Forecast is generated and monitored for any unusual impacts applied.

Judgemental Models

In a business context, we rarely find pure Judgemental Models being used for forecasting, without some sort of base forecast being generated by a Statistical Time Series. This is because the effects of Bias and Human error / "collective think" are too great without some sort of statistics being used to support the Judgemental Model.

As a Judgemental Forecast is based on human judgement, it is affected by some of the limitations of a human being!.
Short Term Accuracy: A Judgement Forecast is mostly accurate and useful over the short term horizon as the human judgement rarely is accurate across long term horizons.
Human Bias: Humans are affected by positive and negative expectations and the Judgement Forecast can easily be swayed based on how the Human is feeling towards the future.
Anchoring: This term means working to a preconceived number or answer. This could be because of the Human Judges most recent experience, expectation or externally influenced (Top Management, peer pressure etc).

For Demand Planning purposes, Judgemental Forecasts may be grouped as below:

Consensus Forecasting: This method involves a collecting feedback from business teams like Sales and Marketing (experts). You may find this described as an Expert Feedback or Delphi method in statistics books but in real business situations this just means aligning your forecast and getting consensus with your internal stakeholders. Most of their feedback is based on their knowledge of the market, advance information or 'gut-feel' and hence qualifies as a Judgemental forecast. Composite Forecasts are another version of this where Forecast is arrived at by taking lower level inputs from various teams or sales persons based on their judgement.

Scenario Forecasting: In Scenario Forecasting a company will usually be working on a long term horizon (typically 3 to 5 years) to create various Forecasting Scenarios based on different factors (Industry, competitor, tax & regulation, environmental and internal). These Forecasts are then reviewed and compared. The Top Management/ Stakeholders then select one of the scenarios to feed into the strategic plan. Most of the Scenario Forecasts are at a high level (category, brand, country etc), as lower level granularity is not very accurate at these long horizons.

Forecasting by Analogy: This method assumes that a products Demand is similar to another product, or group of products. This is mostly used in case of New Products where we have no history. The judgemental part comes in deciding the product or group of products being used as the basis for generating forecast for the new product. In some cases the Forecast for the new product is created as a portion or percentage of the product that is being used as an analogy.

Thought Points....... .

- ☐ Would you use the same model/ forecasting algorithm for a SKU though out its lifetime.
- ☐ In which cases would a company use a single forecasting algorithm for all its products.
- ☐ It is good to change the forecasting model for a sku from time to time.. How would this impact the Historical Forecast stored and forecast accuracy calculations.
- ☐ Why are long term business cycles not used within the forecasting model for operational use.

notes..................

notes..................

notes.................

Chapter 6

Multi-Level Demand Planning

Demand Plans can be (and usually are) generated at different levels of aggregation, in different buckets and across different time horizons based on their purpose. A single company will usually have multiple levels of Forecasts all derived from the same base data.

In all areas of the company, accuracy of forecasting and user-friendliness are common requirements. However, because each organization's focus is unique, planning requirements may vary in the following areas:

- Time horizon of forecasts
- Number of products
- Level of detail (SKU, product family, brand, etc.)
- Volume of explicative information (pricing, display penetration etc)
- Automatic processing vs. interactive simulation
- Periodicity (daily, weekly, quarterly)
- Historical data archival
- Measurements, Tracking and reporting

Rather than generate separate Demand plans independently for all of the organization's needs, it makes sense to instead do multi-level demand planning from a single source and then distribute the different levels of plans to all parties. This ensures that they are all in sync at the time of distribution and also controlled from a single source. It also means efficient utilisation of the organizations resources.

Multi-Level Demand Planning and Forecasting is now provided as a key ability within most Demand Planning Systems. The planner however has to understand the need and the complexity of these multiple levels as very few companies have exactly similar planning level structures.

Demand Planning Units

Most Demand Planning System works with standard units of forecasting consisting of one or more attributes. At the basic level a Demand Planning Unit usually consists of a combination of a Product (or Product Group) and a market (or Market Segment). The exact configuration of the Planning Units is done by an organization depending on the business process and planning requirements.

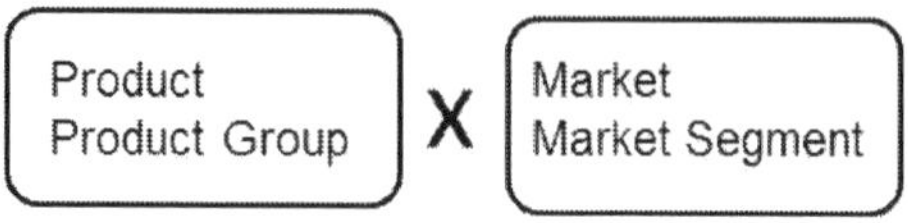

Product Product Group	X	Market Market Segment

The product dimension is usually one of the below (these could be named differently depending on a company's business and preferences):

- Item/Product
- Brand
- Category
- Subcategory
- All Products

The Market dimension is usually one of the below (these could be named differently depending on a company's business and preferences):

- Store
- DC /Warehouse
- Region
- Distribution Channel
- Country

> Note: Some Demand Planning systems allow further configurations of the planning unit into three or even four dimensions, but that can make the systems more complex for the planner to understand and use.

A Demand Planning Unit is usually a combination of the above two dimensions and is an entity for which History can be loaded, forecast created and Demand Planning done. For example a company may decide that their planning unit is an Item at a DC, and in this case they would load History at an Item/DC level and plan and forecast at the same level.

Demand Planning Levels

Most organizations have hierarchies or levels of entities for both their Product as well as their Market Dimension (unless they sell only a single product to a single customer!). Consider the example below for a retailer who may have multiple categories dividing down to subcategories, each of which contains individual products / items.

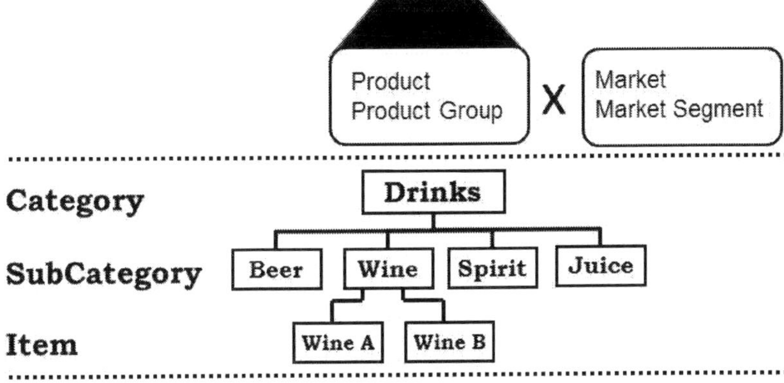

The Retailer could also have a Market Segment Hierarchy with a country having multiple DC's and each DC servicing a group of stores.

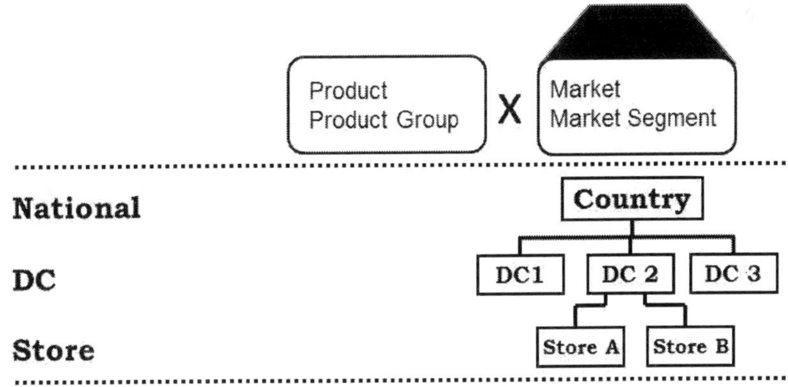

In both the examples above the lowest row defines the lowest and the most Granular level, while the highest level is the most aggregated level. Of course different organizations can have different number of levels of their hierarchies based on how they look at their business.

The Planning Hierarchies can then be a combination of the two dimensions above and the retailer could choose any combination of these depending on what was the objective of the Demand Planning team. In this example there could be nine possible Planning Levels as can be seen from the diagram below (the arrows showing the various combinations possible):

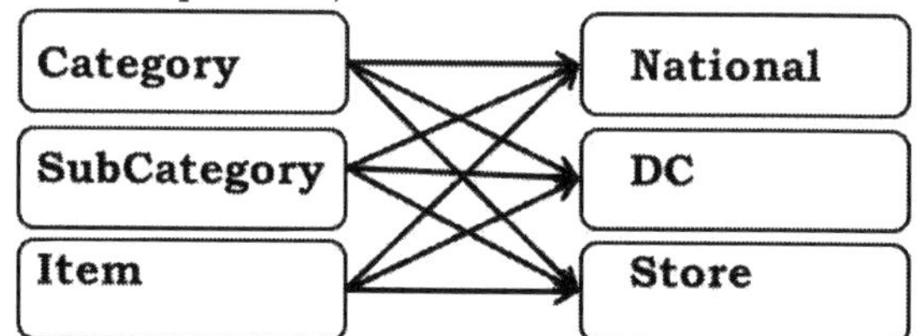

Of course most organizations opting for Multi-Level Demand Planning would use only a few of these as required by their business process. In our example, the organization could have chosen to plan at a single level or Multiple Levels:

Single Level Planning: In this case the organization would select a single Planning level, for example, An Item at a DC level. History Data would then be loaded for each Item at DC level and Forecasts and Plans generated at the same level. There would be no possibility of planning, viewing or reporting the plans or data at any other aggregate or Granular levels. This is adopted by companies who have very limited requirements from Demand Planning:

- Generate DC level Demand Plans for placing orders on Suppliers
- Demand Planning in case of a single DC.
- Demand Planning to model warehousing and Transporting needs.

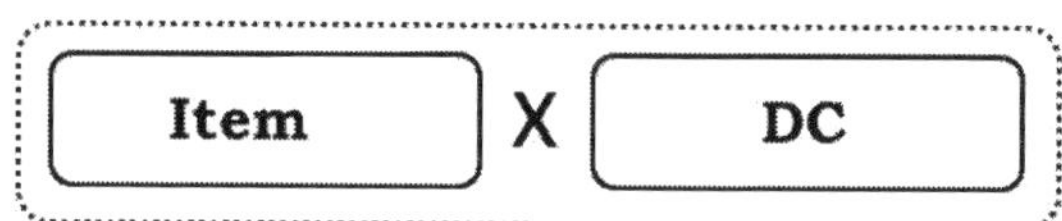

Multi-Level Planning: In this case the organization could select multiple levels. As a simple case, the retailer could plan to create a additional Planning Level for An Item at National level. History Data could then be loaded for each Item at DC level and Forecasts and Plans generated at the DC level as before. The Retailer however, now has the ability to aggregate both History and the Forecast up to Item National Level for aggregated level planning. This is a very simple two level example but quite a few organizations end up creating many more levels because they need aggregated data to support their Business Processes.

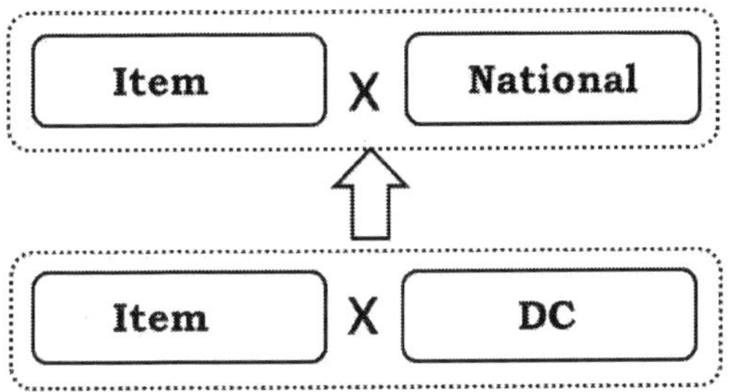

This is adopted by companies who have very complex requirements from Demand Planning. Some of these requirements could be:

- Category or Brand Level Plans to support promotional plans.
- Item, National level aggregate plan for financial /operations planning.
- Store level planning for distribution and deployment of Stocks.
- Item at DC level for Inventory and safety stock planning.

It's also common for organizations to first start with a single level Demand Planning and then graduate to Multi-Level Demand planning once they are comfortable with their Demand Planning systems and have configured their business processes to a single level. For example a retailer could start with an Item at DC level Demand Planning and once the processes are working as desired, rollout the solution to Item at National or Item at Store level. This

'Rolling-Out' would involve creation of additional levels, populating the levels with data and defining new business processes for the additional level.

Forecast Levels

As you may have realised by now selecting and structuring Planning Levels can be a complex exercise and can decide how easy or how hard it will be for the planners to operate your Planning Systems.

The best way to decide your planning levels is to work backwards from the Forecast Levels required to support your business processes. The key focus should be 'Business Process' and not other considerations like reporting or other nice to have features. Too often it is found that the planning levels are configured to support top management expectations of reporting or to enable easy interfacing with other legacy systems which may or may not have data structured correctly to support your business processes.

Given below is a example of how a company could use granular level forecast to aggregate to higher level to support different business needs.

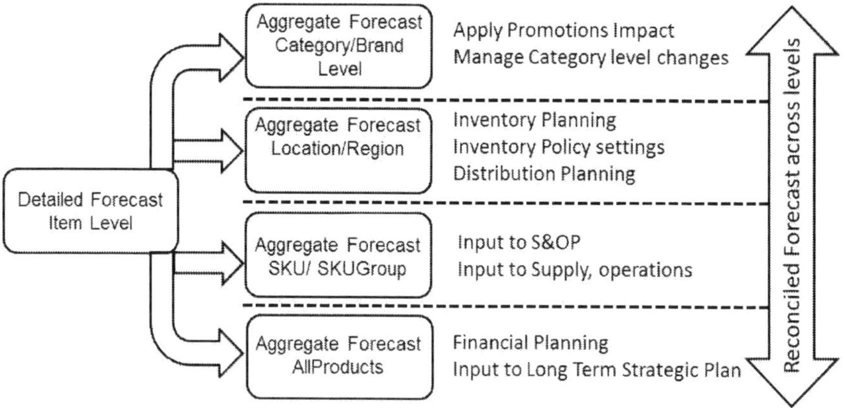

In general, the more simples planning level structures would be easier to maintain and would demand lower resources, while larger number of levels would need complex business process and higher number of resources to operate and maintain your Demand Planning Systems.

It's a trade-off between how much value you want to get out of your Demand Planning teams and systems Vs. what you are willing to invest in terms of resources and costs.

Criteria for creating a Level

The following criteria may be used to decide if a Level needs to be created within your Demand Planning System. Ask yourself the following questions:

- **Would the Demand Planner work at this level?** It doesn't make sense to create a Level just to maintain data or because the data coming from your ERP systems is more granular or aggregate than needed for Demand Planning. If needed you should move the data from your ERP system into an intermediate processing or staging area (database), convert it to the required aggregation (or disaggregation) and then load into your Demand Planning Systems.

- **Do we need output at this level?** In some cases the planner may not work at a level but you may require the output to be aggregated (or disaggregated) to the level before it can be used by other planning systems.

- **Do we plan to load History at this level?** Some Levels may be created for special needs with a limited amount of Data. For example a company may not load or Aggregate History to a Aggregate Level but create the Level for converting Forecast into Pallet cases or for financial planning.

- **Do we plan to generate Forecast at this level?** If there is no Forecast generated (or aggregated) at a level, we need to seriously review the need of creating the level. In most cases such levels may be required only to support workarounds or Historical Data purposes and as such they are most probably not required within your planning system.

- **How Many Planning Items would result by adding this level?** In some cases the performance (and speed) of your Demand Planning system may be affected if very large number of Planning Units are created for a level. This can happen at very granular levels and should be avoided unless absolutely necessary. For example a retailer with 1000 stores and 2000 products can potentially have two million Planning Units if they decided to create a Item at a Store Level.

- **Would the Aggregated data be used for Reporting only?** One of the things that should be kept in mind is that your Demand Planning System is a Planning System first, any other need like reporting should be considered secondary and reviewed in case they have an adverse effect on the Planning ability of the systems. Any request to create additional levels in the planning system for reporting purposes or to support the needs of other reporting systems should be seriously reviewed. More dangerous than an aggregated level is, if there is a need to create a lower (more granular) level just for reporting needs.

- **Would the Aggregated data be used infrequently?** In some cases there may be a request / suggestion for creating additional levels to support ad-hoc or specialised scenarios which cannot be handled by your regular Demand Planning Setup. An example could be a specific customer who refuses to place orders at your SKU / SKUGroup levels and places orders for a different aggregation level. In this case it would be incorrect to just create a new level in your Demand Planning System to support the loading/ input of customer orders from this specific customer. Instead it may be better to do this outside the system (or negotiate with the customer for the correct level of data) and then load it at the right level.

Another example could be creating a level to support Christmas or a specific major event. Again this should be handled using standardised processes and scenarios rather than create additional levels.

- **Would the planning items have to be maintained manually?** One key criteria is to evaluate if planning items at a particular level would need any Manual (Planner) maintenance, setup, overrides etc. This could directly lead to additional workload for the Planners and put a strain on Resources and Time. Of course the reverse is true as well, the Planners could be doing a load of manual activities which would be taken away or made easier by just adding a new data level. A net impact in terms of Hours/ Minutes per planner need to be estimated for creating a level in this case.

Considerations for Multilevel Demand Planning

The following key points need to be taken into consideration while putting in place a multi-level setup for Demand Planning. Of course not all of these may be applicable for all Organizations as it depends on the Demand Planning Solution used by them:

- **Planning Level**: The Demand Planner should be required to work on a single specified level (Planning Level) for most of his business process scenarios. Any work on levels other than the Planning Level should be by exception. This ensures efficiency in work and reduces any chance of error creeping in due to the different changes made at different levels in case the forecast in not reconciled between levels. It is the usual practice for the Planning Level to be the level at which History is loaded in the system.

- **Forecast Accuracy**: Forecast Accuracy should usually be tracked at the Planning Level (i.e. the default level at which the planner works). This also makes sense as the real history is usually imported at this level. Of course the organization may want to track accuracy at aggregate levels as well, but its best to do this outside the Demand Planning System using reporting and data mining tools.

- **History Loading Level**: The decision of the level at which to load History is a key one and affects the final output of Demand Planning. Forecast cannot be generated within Demand Planning systems at a more granular level than the History loaded, without using approximations of ratios to split the forecast down. It's also usual practice to load History only at one level (and from one source).

- **Synchronisation of Levels**: The more the number of levels, the higher is the effort required to maintain the different levels and the relationships, links or mapping between the levels. As a new product is created or a product deleted at one of the levels, there may be manual work or system configuration required to be done at all levels to ensure the levels remain valid and in synchronisation. The process of synchronisation should be defined well before the levels are created to ensure it fits within the Business Process.

- **Granular levels**: Granular and very low levels should be avoided in Demand Planning unless there is a critical requirement to work at that level. Demand Planning by its very definition, is at aggregate levels and should not be confused with need for granular levels either for reporting or Supply/Operations.

- **Resources / Planner**: Each additional level will add to planner workload due to exception management, issues resolution, setup and maintenance. It follows that if you have limited resources or time constraints, you should look to minimise your levels to the most critical ones required to support your business process.

- **Conversions:** once the levels and their usage have been decided the next key step is to decide the Units and Time Buckets for the aggregate levels. In some cases you may find that converting the data using factors / prices etc generates more useful levels, while in other cases you may want to have a level with different time buckets to support your planning requirements.

- **Naming conventions**: It's important to agree and decide how the names of the Planning Units at higher level will be structured. It's easy to do this at the SKU level where most companies just use the same codes as used in their source systems or transaction systems, but at aggregate levels you may find that the names are used differently in different systems. It's also possible that no real codes are allocated to higher levels. For example at SKU level an item may have a code like 180011, but at sub category level it may be called White Wines. The company would then need to decide whether they want their higher level to be named as White Wines or use some code like WW1001 etc. The same would be applicable for different levels of Markets, channels, locations etc.

- **Maximum number of levels**: Lastly you may want to specify a maximum number of levels allowed to all teams within your Demand Planning community. For example in case you have multiple business or countries covered within your company you could define the maximum number of levels at a corporate demand planning level and leave the structure of the planning items to be configured by the local teams.

History and Forecast Aggregation

History is usually loaded into your Demand Planning Systems at a single level. In case of Multi-Level Demand Planning, Forecast may also be generated at a single or multiple levels. Aggregation for both History and Forecast may be in the following ways:

- **Simple Aggregation:** In this case History or Forecast is aggregated to higher levels by just summing the lower levels and creating a aggregated history for higher level planning items using predefined linkages or maps. This may be done when lower level history is not robust or is patchy for some products which do not sell very frequently. For example if a retailer plans at Item Store level and finds that there are some products which are sold infrequently at a store level , He can decide to aggregate the history of the product across all Stores and then generate a forecast. In this case the retailer has a better chance of getting a robust and usable history than planning at the store level.

> Note: Not all Demand Planning Systems may support Aggregation to higher levels. In some cases it may need processing of data before it is loaded within your system. The Aggregation concept should however make you aware of the various possibilities and how they can help support your business process.

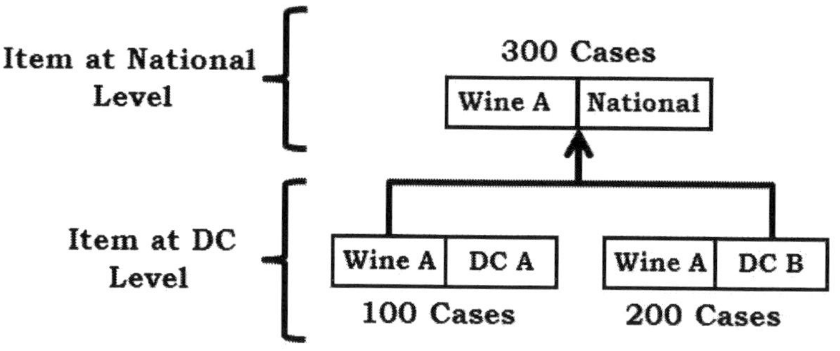

A Simple History Aggregation example

- **Time Aggregation:** In some cases, demand may not be very patchy (contain zero values) when observed in shorter time buckets. For example if a manufacturer ships on a weekly or biweekly basis from a DC , the daily demand patterns are going to look very patchy but the weekly aggregated data will be more robust for demand planning purposes. Similarly in some cases weekly data may look patchy for some products or categories and it may make better sense to aggregate the Demand to monthly or four weekly buckets to really get a good history for forecasting.

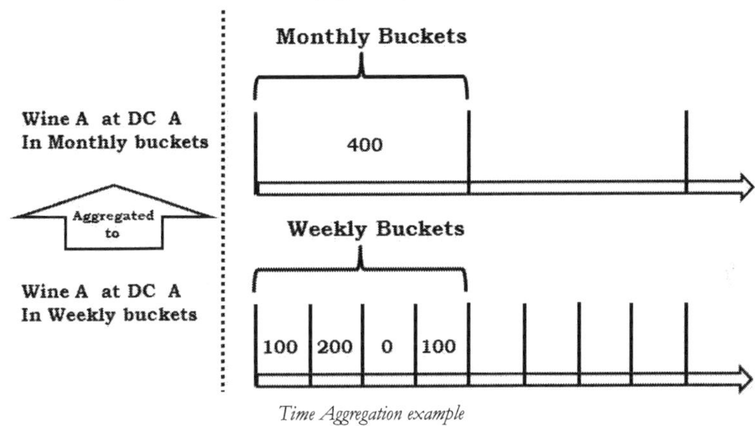

Time Aggregation example

Time Aggregation is also useful in capturing trends that may not be clearly visible at more granular levels. Shown below is the same data in weekly and monthly buckets. Notice how the trend is more clearly defined in the monthly buckets.

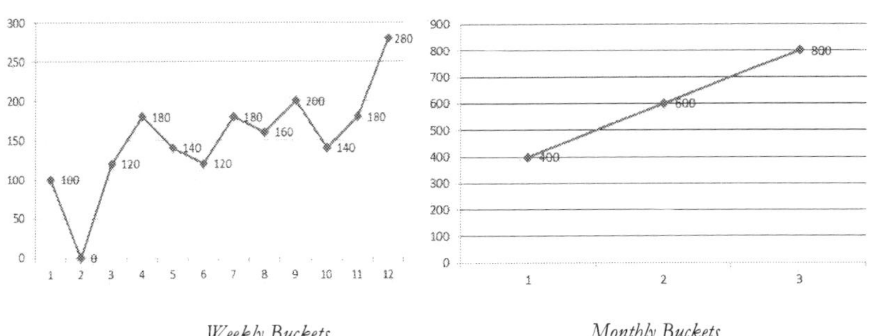

Weekly Buckets *Monthly Buckets*

- **Factored Aggregation:** In some cases you may want to create aggregated History or forecast at a higher level in different units. This is usually done with the use of factors that are multiplied at the time of aggregation. This is done automatically in case of most Demand Planning Systems, but the planner needs to be aware of how this type of aggregation can be used.

  Some of the cases where this is usually done are:
  - Conversion to Value: This needs prices to be loaded in addition to the History data. The historical quantities (or forecast quantities) are multiplied with the prices to generate the aggregated converted data. This may be needed by your financial teams to compare against their planned targets.
  - Conversion to Weight: This may be needed by your manufacturing and operations teams to plan production or order key raw materials.
  - Conversion to Space: This may be needed for computing warehousing space needed for the forecasted volumes.
  - Conversion to Pallets: This may be needed for transport planning based on the number of pallets planned to be moved.
  - Conversion to Multipacks : This may be needed in case you plan sales targets or promotions volumes in multipacks (packs of multiple products in a single multipack, as in a 6 pack of beer)

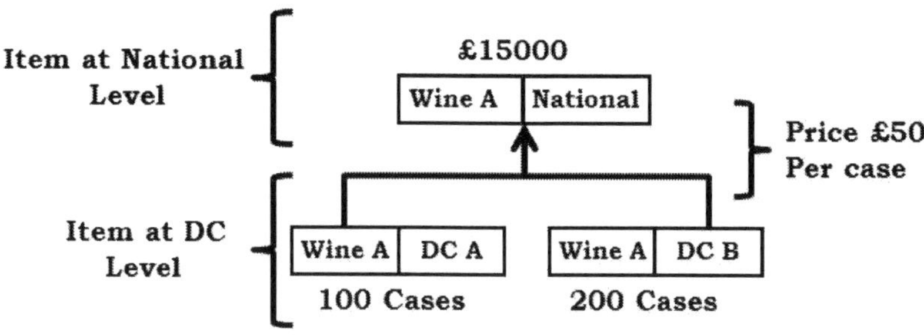

Aggregation example with Conversion Factors

- **Component Aggregation:** Both History as well as Forecast usually have their time series data stored as separate components. Most demand planning systems allow you to store one or more of the following types of History data:

History
- Total History
- Base History
- Promotions History
- System Identified Historical Outliers

One or more of these components may be stored for every SKU/ Planning Item / Level in your Demand Planning System based on how the data is loaded from your ERP systems. Given below is an example where Raw History is imported from your ERP system and split into Base and Promoted History (either by the system or manually). In this example we would get three components of History stored for an Item A at DC A and DC B separately. Component Aggregation in this case will mean that we decide to aggregate just one component of the History to an aggregate level (In this example it's Base History).

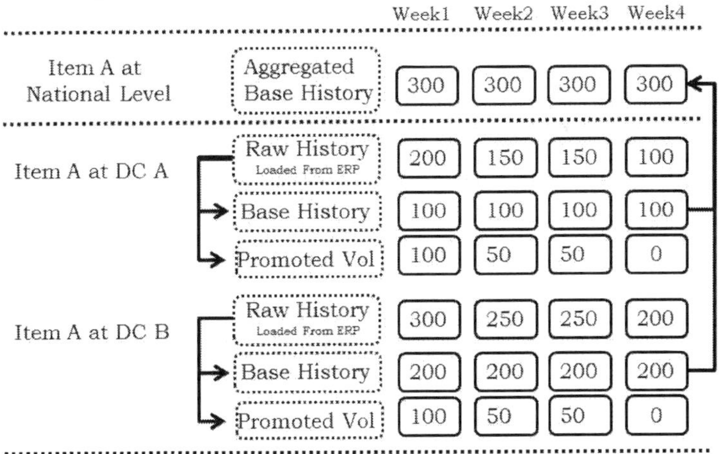

History Component Aggregation example

Most demand planning systems will also allow you to store one or more of the following types of Forecast Component data:

Forecast

- Total Forecast
- Base Forecast
- Forecasted Promotions Uplift
- Other Market Intelligence
- Future Sales Targets
- Other values (different systems may have different options)

Continuing from our previous example, if Item A at National level has a base forecast of 300 per week (in line with its Base History of 300 per week), we can imagine a case where its forecast is aggregated with other products forecasts at National level to generate a Brand level Base forecast for the Brand under which Item A lies. This could then be used for making Brand Level plans in case the company manages budgets, trade allowances or promotions at Brand level (for example).

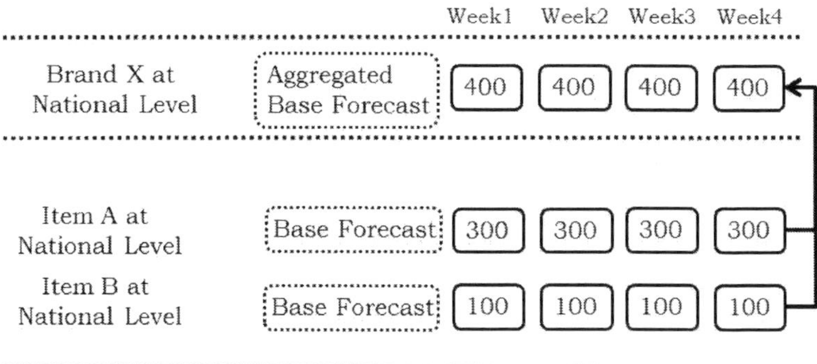

Forecast Component Aggregation example

Forecast Reconciliation

As a company starts using multiple levels and aggregations of forecast, there is a risk that the data at different levels can get misaligned due to modifications / adjustments made at these levels. It's also possible that the company generates forecasts at different levels using aggregated and granular history. A consistent view of data is then essential to ensure that everyone is talking the same numbers. The process of maintaining equality between total forecast at these multiple levels is known as Forecast Reconciliation. This is usually the last step in the Demand Planning process before the forecast numbers are published to other teams and would be performed at least once during a week (in case of a weekly Demand Planning Cycle).Most Demand Planning Systems that allow multi-level Demand Planning support some processes for reconciliation. Two approaches to forecast reconciliation are usually used:

- **Top-Down Reconciliation:** In case of Top-Down approach the Forecast for the higher level is assumed to be correct and the forecast at the lower level is adjusted (increased / decreased) accordingly. The allocation of the balance component at the higher level (plus or minus) is spread to the lower level linked items using proportional ratios. These ratios may either be the ratio of their base forecast, the ratio of their historical actual sales, or equal proportions spread to all items.

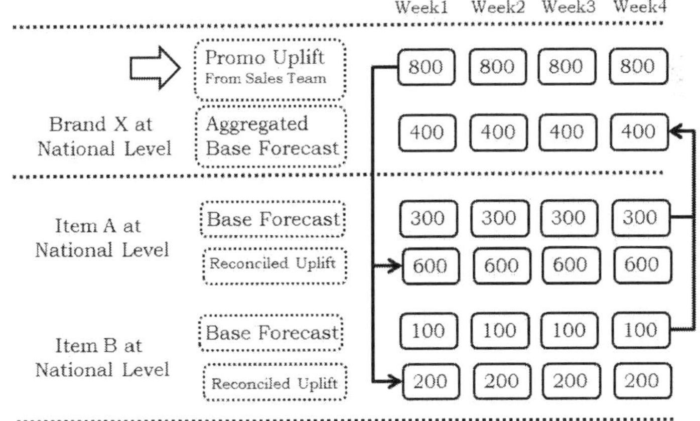

Top-Down Reconciliation example

- **Bottom-Up Reconciliation:** In case of Bottom-Up approach the Forecast for the lower level is assumed to be correct and the forecast at the higher level is adjusted (increased / decreased) accordingly. The difference between Bottom-Up reconciliation and simple aggregation is that in Bottom-Up reconciliation just the balance component is aggregated upwards while in simple aggregation all of the forecast components are aggregated to the higher level. So the end result (total Forecast) at the higher level will be the same in both cases.

  You would follow Bottom-Up reconciliation if you were generating forecast separately at the higher level. In this case a simple aggregation would have replaced the higher level forecast. In case no higher level forecast was being generated separately you would follow a simple aggregation approach.

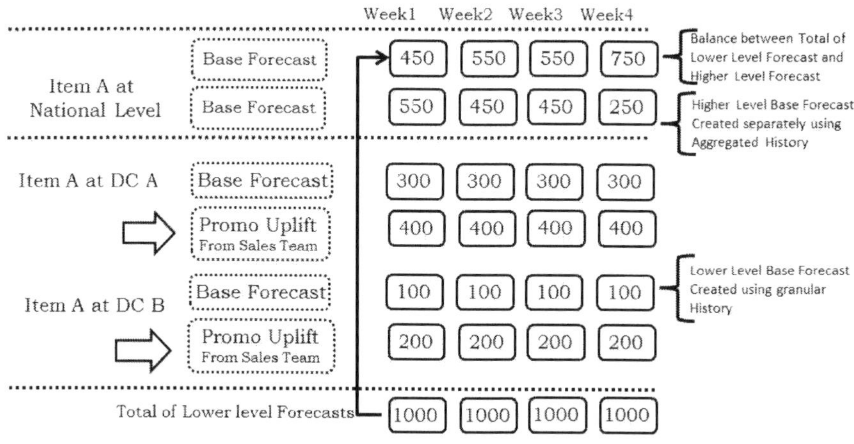

History Component Aggregation example

In the example above the sum of all forecasts is taken for all lower level items and compared against the forecast at the Higher level linked to them. The balance forecast is then created as an additional reconciled forecast at the higher level.

Aggregation Tips

Aggregation and Multi-Level Demand Planning is usually applied in the following cases:

- Lower level data is patchy (lots of zero History values).
- History volumes are low (very low quantities).
- Very Volatile History (sharp peaks and troughs).
- Promotions volumes available only at higher levels.
- Business Process requires planners to work at multiple levels.

Aggregate level planning has the following benefits:

- Easier to manage history and Forecast
- Generates more accurate forecasts and plans
- Less volume of Data generated
- Less resources and planners needed

But there are constraints as well:

- Less useful for short term operational planning
- Output needs to be broken down to lower levels to be used
- Synchronisation issues between different levels
- Increase in data volume due to multiple levels
- Additional workload generated for planners

It is recommended that companies treat the definition of levels as an important stage and decide on the levels after a detailed analysis of:

- Workload Generated
- Data Sources
- Data Conversions
- Data Maintenance
- Business Process around the different levels
- System capability to support multiple levels
- Training needs and planner learning curves

Reconciliation Tips

Reconciliation in Demand Planning is usually applied in the following cases:

- Multiple Level Demand Planning.
- Links defined between multiple levels.
- Different total forecast at different levels.

Reconciling Forecasts has the following benefits:

- Demand Plans are synchronised between different levels.
- Forecasts can be generated at separate levels from History.
- Planners can plan at any of the multiple levels.
- Transparency and visibility of reconciled component of forecasts
- Reconciliation can be positive or negative. (i.e. can increase or decrease forecast.).

But there are constraints as well:

- Only two levels can be reconciled at a single time. In case of more than two levels the forecast would need to be reconciled multiple times.
- History is usually not reconciled because in most cases the total History doesn't change. In case of component aggregation, the History is deliberately kept different at separate levels and reconciliation would not make sense in this case as well.
- Reconciliation assumes that there is forecast at both the higher and lower levels.

Other points related to Reconciliation:

- Reconciliation is usually supported as an automated process by most Demand Planning Systems with Multi-Level Demand Planning capabilities.
- Reconciliation may also be done between:
    - Your companies forecast and your customers forecast
    - Your Financial forecast and Demand Forecast
    - Your sales targets and your Demand Forecast

Thought Points........

- [ ] How is Multi-Level Demand Planning different from Single Level Demand Planning.
  In which business cases would you use Multi-Level Demand Planning.
- [ ] What are the different types of Aggregation.
  How would you use Aggregation to create a Demand Plan in financial values.
- [ ] What criteria would you use to define the default level at which your planner will work most of the time.
  What impacts can multiple levels of Demand Planning have on Planner Workload.
- [ ] What defines the lowest and the highest level of planning you should create.
  What are the issues with having very granular levels for Demand Planning.

notes.............

notes..................

notes..................

Chapter 7

Demand Planning for New Products

Demand Planning for new products is very different from planning for existing products. The following points will give you an insight into the difficulties faced by planners:

- New Products don't have any History
- Demand Estimates and Plans may be needed well before the New Product Launch Date.
- New Products don't exist in most systems before they are launched.
- New Products need much more manual input than standard existing products.
- The forecast Accuracy for new products is mostly low doe to the constantly changing volume levels.
- Most Retailers and Manufacturers have to continuously release a large number of new products to keep innovating and to keep the competition at bay. New Products may need a prebuild of inventory requiring Demand and Distribution planning well before the product is launched.
- The New product has to be manually flagged to be removed from the New Product stage in most planning systems and may need additional setup to be regularised as a standard product.

The bottom-line is that while New Products may be critical to continued business growth and to keep the company's product portfolio fresh and interesting to the customer, it generates a large amount of additional workload for the Demand Planner (as well as Sales and Marketing) and the Planner needs to be aware of the various options to address the requirements of Marketing and sales. New Product Introductions need much more collaboration between Demand Planners and Sales/Marketing as the Demand needs to much more responsive to changes in case of New Products.

Stages of a Product Life Cycle

Most products have to go through similar lifecycles of getting introduced to the market, entering a growth phase of rapid sales, entering a stable rate of sales till the sales of the product start flagging and declining. This chapter will focus just on the New product introduction phase, but it's good to have a brief summary of the differences in the four stages from a Demand Planning perspective:

- **New Introduction Phase**: In the Introduction Phase the company focuses on making the customers aware of the new product and its benefits / key attributes. Availability is critical at new product launch time and the company also makes efforts to get more customers to try the new product through Marketing, Advertising, Packaging and product placement. Some companies may have done a customer survey, market research or a trial pilot run of the product before its launch. The Demand Planner plays a critical role during the new product phase:

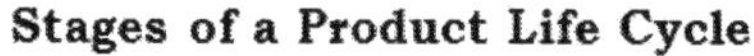

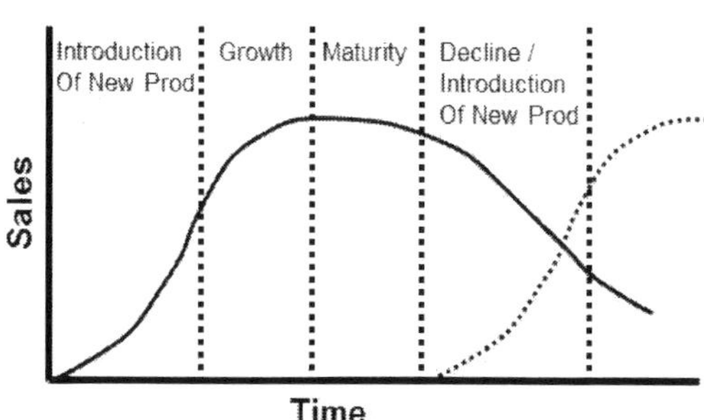

  - Setup new product in Demand Planning System
  - Identify Demand Planning Approach to be used
  - Create Initial Demand Plans
  - Collaborate with Marketing and Sales to get Aggregate Level Demand Targets /Plans
  - Track Actual sales with Forecast and adjust Forecast accordingly
  - Identify Like Products

- Create Launch Profiles
- Coordinate with Supply to ensure they have forecast Data to prebuild inventory
- Participate in S&OP Meetings and take action based on decisions agreed.

- **Growth Phase**: The focus in this phase is market growth and adoption of the new product by consumers. Availability is still critical and the company may maintain an above normal level of safety stocks to guarantee customer service / availability. The products may be promoted in this phase together market share and increase growth rates. The Demand Planner has the following role in this phase:
    - Modify Parameters and Algorithm used for Demand Planning if required.
    - Continuously Track Forecast Accuracy and inform if there is a downward or upward trend.
    - If the New Product has accumulated enough history (at least six months), the planner may decide to start using its own history instead of using estimates or manual inputs.
    - Remove any new product profiles that were attached to shape the initial demand curve as they may no longer be applicable.
    - Most companies will have a defined time period when they will consider a new product to have moved out of the new product phase and into the growth phase. (for example six months).

- **Maturity Phase**: In the Maturity phase the growth in sales diminishes. The upwards sales trends stabilize and become flatter, and there may even be a downward trend. Depending on the industry this could happen from a year to many years from product launch. There may even be industries where products have very short lifecycles and get phased out even before they reach this stage. Invariably, by the time the new products have reached the maturity phase a majority of the new products may have be pruned and only the strongest products may survive. These are however, most likely to be the bread and butter for your company. Once the product reaches maturity phase some advanced demand planning systems may signal off exceptions as they note distinct trend changes. The Demand Planner has the following role during this phase:

- Cleanse History
- Manage and Resolve exceptions
- Add Promotions Uplift Forecasts
- Aggregate and Reconcile Forecast
- Review Demand Trend and seasonality

- **Decline and New Introduction Phase**: During this phase, the product has a downward trend and may be losing market share and sales. The following approaches are usually taken by companies for products in this phase:
    - Relaunch product: This may involve repackaging, changing product attributes (colour taste etc), repricing or using alternate channels.
    - Replace Product: The Company can decide to replace the product with a new variant or another product addressing the same market. In case of replacement both products may be available for a short period of time till the inventories of the product being replaced have been liquidated. Some companies may sell off the existing inventories for the product being replaced as markdowns.
    - Discontinue Product: The company may decide to discontinue the product altogether.

The Demand Planner has the following role to play in this phase:

- Execute steps to discontinue product
- Delete /remove the product and associated data from the Demand Planning Systems. The planner may want to archive or maintain History in case it's planned to be used for a replacement product.

- Ensure all stakeholders are informed about the discontinuation in case a previous forecast for the product has already been published.
- In case of a replacement product, the planner needs to execute the new product business process for the replacement product.

In most cases the Demand Planners role starts well before the launch of the New Product (usually 18 to 12 weeks before the launch date) as he has to provides estimates of Demand, coordinate with Marketing and Sales on launch dates, replacement products etc, coordinate with IS/ IT to ensure the new product is created in the Master Data and flows through to the Demand Planning Systems and then perform his New Product Introduction Scenarios in the Demand Planning System.

Types of New Product Introduction Scenarios

The following key points need to be taken into consideration while putting in place a multi-level setup for Demand Planning. Of course not all of these may be applicable for all Organizations as it depends on the Demand Planning Solution used by them:

- **Replace Existing Product**: In case of replacement of a new product the key activity is to ensure the new product replaces the correct existing product in the Demand Planning System. It is sometimes possible that the new product may be replacing multiple existing products. The Demand Planner needs to coordinate with Marketing and sales to confirm these products. The Demand Planner also needs to have clarity on the Launch Date of the New Product and the Discontinuation Date of the existing product (Products) being replaced. It's not necessary that both these dates be the same. There may be an overlap in the dates in some cases .The Demand Planner can then use the

History of the Existing Product to drive the initial Demand Planning of the New Product being introduced.

- **New Product in Existing Market**: In this case a New Product in introduced to the existing market of the company without discontinuing another product. There is just an addition of a New Product to the product portfolio. Even in this case it's very rare that the New Product will be totally dissimilar to existing products. Most of the time the new product would be a variant of an existing product created to address a market need that was not being satisfied by the existing products. There is also a possibility of the new product cannibalizing some of the demand from an existing product (products). The Demand Planner may not have a replaced product to use the history and will have to coordinate with Marketing and Sales to identify products which may be similar to model history. Additionally the Demand Planner may have to setup cannibalizing relationships if applicable.

- **New Product in New Market**: This is a rare case and happens when a new company, category or division is launched or a company enters a new geography, market or country. In such a case the company would most likely have no history of the product or similar products that could be used. Extensive surveys, customer feedback, getting feedback through social media, competitor study, expert assessment and running pilot launches are used by Marketing to get an initial assessment of potential volumes. Marketing then communicates this to the Demand Planning Team who can then create the granular forecasts using launch profiles, lifecycles or by creating manual forecasts. Once the product starts accumulating its own history the forecast is then tuned to follow the history levels achieved.

  The other approach used for these types of new products is diffusion models which are discussed in the next section.

- **Existing Product in New Market**: This happens when a company decides to sell a product in markets/channels/stores where it was not sold earlier. This is common with retailers who may sometimes range their product portfolio across a limited number of stores initially to gauge the customer response and then may range them across all stores. A common approach in this case, is to use history from similar locations/regions or stores, and use the products history there to generate the forecast for the new product.

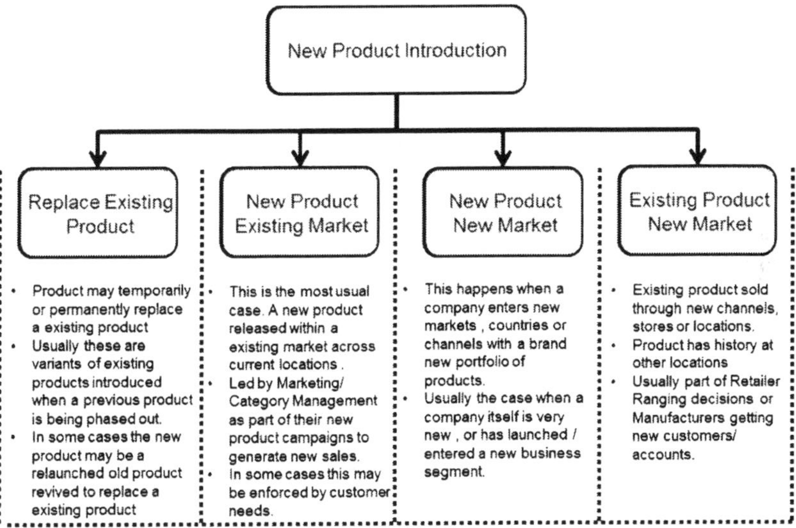

Demand Planning Options for New Products

Options for the Demand Planner to plan for New Products are:

Pseudo-History: The Demand Planner can create artificial history or pseudo-History for the new products and then treat it the same as a regular product. This is usually done when the product is not expected to follow a 'S' Curve for new introduction (either the new product is just replacing an old product or there is no marketing or promotion being done to get the customers to know about the new product).In all of the cases below creating Pseudo-History should be a one off activity before the launch of the new product and not something that would need to be done frequently for the same new product. Key planner activities and decisions in this approach are:

- Identification of a similar product/category/brand.
- Identification of a similar location/ store/region.
- Decisions on the New Product launch date.
- Decision on discontinuation of any replaced products.

Once all of the above are clarified, the planner can then decide which approach to take to create the pseudo-History. The approaches below could be used by the planner as a one of manual exercise by exporting and importing data into the Demand Planning System, or it's possible that the Demand Planning system being used provides these functionalities as a semi-automated process based on planner selection:

- **Copy History for new product**: This can be done if the new product is expected to be very similar to an existing product. The planner can copy the history as it is or decide to scale it up or down depending on how the new product is expected to sell. The planner may also create a manual override for a prelaunch buffer for the new product. It's also essential that the planner keep track of where the history has been copied from and which new products are using copied History in case the process needs to be reversed or History deleted once the new product has accumulated its own history.

- **Copy History for new location**: This can also be done if it's an existing product being sold in a new store /location or to a new customer. In this case the planner can decide to copy history for the same product from another store/location/region which has similar attributes (size, potential market, demography etc) as the new store or market. In case no such location/store/region is found the planner may use the closest match and then decide to scale the history up or down. The planner could also create a manual uplift for building up buffer for the product launch or apply a short term profile if the demand planning tool has the functionality.

- **Copy Historical profiles/patterns/seasonality**: In some cases the planner may feel that the volumes of the new product may be comparable to one product, while the expected profile/pattern/seasonality of sales for the new product is expected to follow another product. In such cases the planner may want to extract historical patterns/ seasonality from one product and the sales volumes from another and create a composite sales History. Some advanced Demand Planning systems may offer this as a standard functionality based on user selected products.

- **Use Aggregated History**: Consider a case where two regions are being merged, or where two small stores are being closed and a larger one being created in its place. In such (and similar) cases the products that are sold at the new store can be considered to be as New Products as they will not have any history at the new store. The planner can just aggregate the history for the locations that have been closed and use this is the history for the new store. The planner can also scale the history up or down based on other attributes of the new store. There may be an uplift at the opening of the new store which can be added by the planner as well.

- **Merge History**: This is a similar case to the above with the difference that history of multiple products at the same location is merged together to create a history for the new product being introduced. Again, this may happen if the new product is replacing multiple products. The planner can also scale the new product history, up or down if required.

Manual Input: In some cases the Planner may decide to use manual input for creating forecast for a new product, rather than create Pseudo-History. This might either happen when there is no usable data for History or the planner does not want to tamper with history. The planner needs to coordinate with the sales and marketing teams to get the data below:

- Average sales of the product per week
- Expected shape of demand curve immediately after launch.
- Duration after which the new product sales is expected to be stabilized.

The Demand Planner can then follow one of the approaches below:

- **Manually create flatline Forecast**: In this approach a flatline forecast is created (either manually or supported by application or batch jobs) equal to the average sales for the new product expected. This is usually done for new products that are not expected to generate large volumes and are just additions to a portfolio. A variation of this is the stepped flatline, where there is a stepped increase or decrease to the forecast after a time period. Some Demand Planning applications support the generation of a manual forecast using specified Level and Trend to generate a forecast which is not flatline.
- **Copy Forecast from existing product**: One option the Planner has is to copy forecast from a like item manually instead of copying History. This has the advantage of not creating any artificial history or dummy data, but needs to be done on a regular basis as the base forecast for the existing product is updated.
- **Create Launch Profile with Mean**: This is provided as functionality by many demand planning systems but can also be done outside the system for generating forecast. This is most useful in case new products are launched frequently and the same profile needs to be used multiple times.

Diffusion Models: The Bass Diffusion Model developed by Prof Frank Bass in 1969 is mostly applicable to New Product Introduction for consumer durable products, consumer electronics etc (fashion clothing, mobile phones etc). These products are characterised by a limited maximum demand with multiple competitors in the market.

The Bass Diffusion model generates a forecast which is derived from two factors within a specified maximum potential demand for the product. The first factor generates an estimated impact on the demand due to advertisement or direct marketing to grow awareness about the product. The second factor is the likelihood of a potential customer becoming a customer based on word-of-mouth endorsements, social media or plain imitation of the first group. This model needs inputs from the Demand Planner related to the estimated total potential demand for a new product. The rate of expected diffusion or adoption of the product due to company's advertisement and other efforts and the rate at which existing customers/users are expected to spread the demand though word-of-mouth etc.

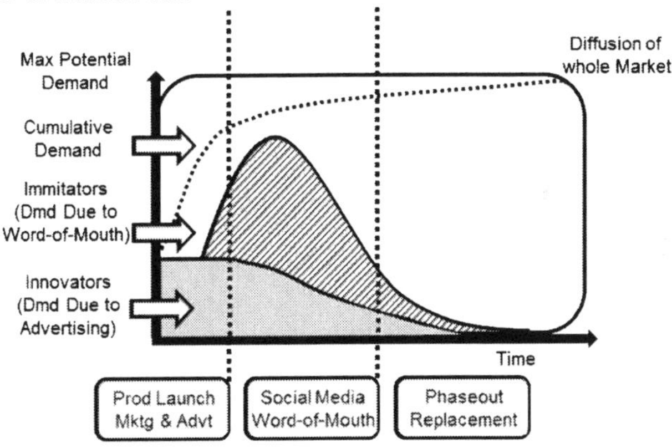

The Bass's Basement Research Institute is a not-for-profit institute and you can visit their website at www.bassbasement.org for details and examples.

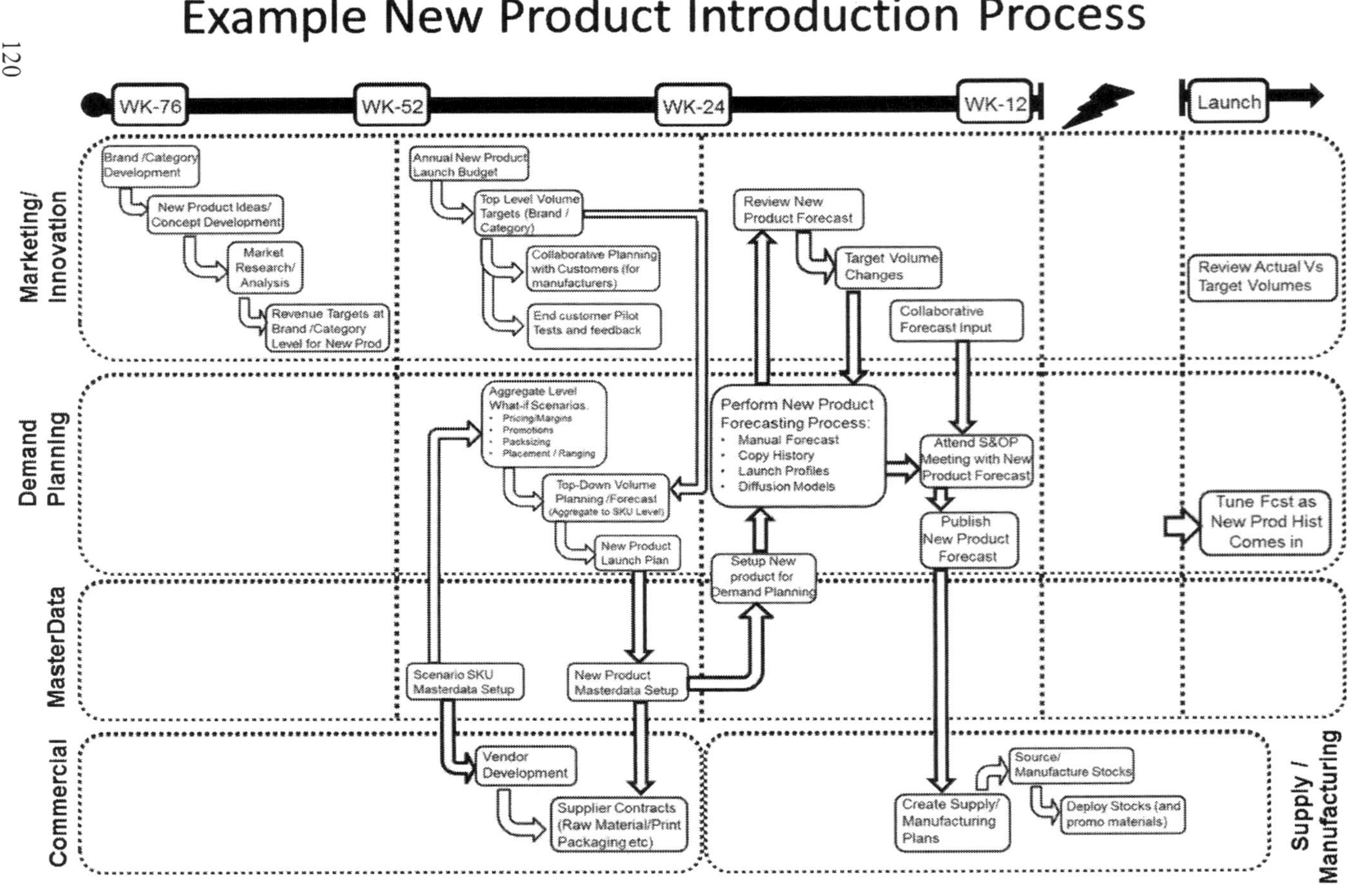
Example New Product Introduction Process
WK-76
WK-52
WK-24
WK-12
Launch
Marketing/ Innovation
Demand Planning
MasterData
Commercial
Supply / Manufacturing
Brand /Category Development
New Product Ideas/ Concept Development
Market Research/ Analysis
Revenue Targets at Brand /Category Level for New Prod
Annual New Product Launch Budget
Top Level Volume Targets (Brand / Category)
Collaborative Planning with Customers (for manufacturers)
End customer Pilot Tests and feedback
Review New Product Forecast
Target Volume Changes
Collaborative Forecast Input
Review Actual Vs Target Volumes
Aggregate Level What-if Scenarios.
Pricing/Margins
Promotions
Packsizing
Placement / Ranging
Top-Down Volume Planning /Forecast (Aggregate to SKU Level)
New Product Launch Plan
Perform New Product Forecasting Process:
Manual Forecast
Copy History
Launch Profiles
Diffusion Models
Attend S&OP Meeting with New Product Forecast
Publish New Product Forecast
Tune Fcst as New Prod Hist Comes in
Scenario SKU Masterdata Setup
New Product Masterdata Setup
Setup New product for Demand Planning
Vendor Development
Supplier Contracts (Raw Material/Print Packaging etc)
Create Supply/ Manufacturing Plans
Source/ Manufacture Stocks
Deploy Stocks (and promo materials)

Thought Points....... .

- [ ] How is Demand Planning for New Products different from Planning for regular products.
  What is the Demand Planners role in planning New Products.

- [ ] What are the different stages of a product's Lifecycle.
  Do all products go through all of these stages.

- [ ] What are the various ways a Demand Planner can create History for a New Product.
  What should be done to the Pseudo-History once the New Product has history of its own.

- [ ] What are the different stakeholders that are involved in launching a new product in an organization.
  What roles do they play.

notes.................

notes..................

notes.................

Chapter 8

Planning Promotions Impact

Promotions are usually price incentives to customers to buy more of your company's products. This is standard practice even though most companies are aware that promotions usually just end in pulling demand forward instead of creating additional demand. There is an observed dip in demand immediately after the end of a promotion for most products. The end result may be a reduced margin across the promoted and non-promoted periods when taken as a whole. Some of the reasons the promotions happen at all are:

- The promoted product may be an incentive to drive more customers in through your doors with the hope that they buy additional products
- Products may be promoted to encourage changes in habits in consumers and to encourage them to try new products.
- Products may be promoted to generate additional demand and drive new customers to you with the hope that they stay with you after the promotion is ended.
- Products may be promoted to get rid of old stocks.
- Products may be promoted when there is limited demand or demand for a limited period (as there is minimal risk of a dip after the promotion)
- Products may be promoted to increase Brand Awareness.
- Products may be promoted where the cost of the promotion or price incentive is either shared or completely borne by the suppliers. The suppliers in turn may be funding it to increase their efficiencies of scale, utilise unused capacity to get rid of excess stock/ inventory.
- Products may be promoted where the original price has a large amount of margin and even after the promotion the company ends up making a substantial margin.
- Products may be promoted to discourage competition and act as a barrier to entry into the market.

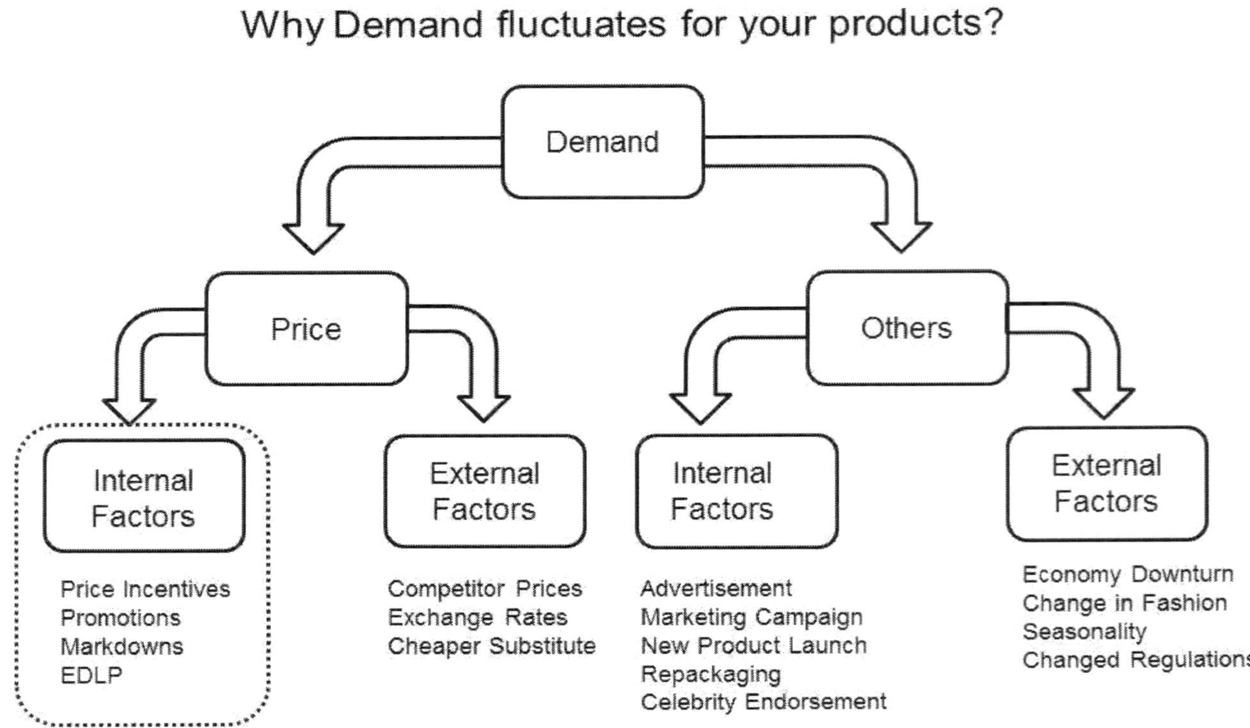
Why Demand fluctuates for your products?
Demand
Price
Others
Internal Factors
Price Incentives
Promotions
Markdowns
EDLP
External Factors
Competitor Prices
Exchange Rates
Cheaper Substitute
Internal Factors
Advertisement
Marketing Campaign
New Product Launch
Repackaging
Celebrity Endorsement
External Factors
Economy Downturn
Change in Fashion
Seasonality
Changed Regulations

A Demand Planner has two main options for planning Promotional Uplifts.

- **Coordinate with Sales Teams** to get their estimated Promotional Volumes for planned future promotions. This has the obvious drawbacks of depending on Sales for the Forecast while the Planner has to own the final forecast. An approach that is usually suggested here is to provide the Base Forecast to the sales teams at SKU and aggregated levels where promotions are applied and then get the promotional volume estimates. An additional step that can be performed here is to give sales input on the promotional volumes achieved for the same SKUs or product groups during historical promoted periods for comparison. The planner of course needs to constantly challenge the Promotional estimated volumes to understand their basis otherwise the natural tendency of the sales team will generate a positive bias to the forecast. This approach also has the drawback of short term vision. The Sales Team will naturally have more clarity and focus the immediate Promotions than the Long Term ones. This also means that there will be very frequent changes to Promotional Uplift Volumes (almost on a weekly basis) as the Sales Team accumulates more and more input to arrive at their estimates.

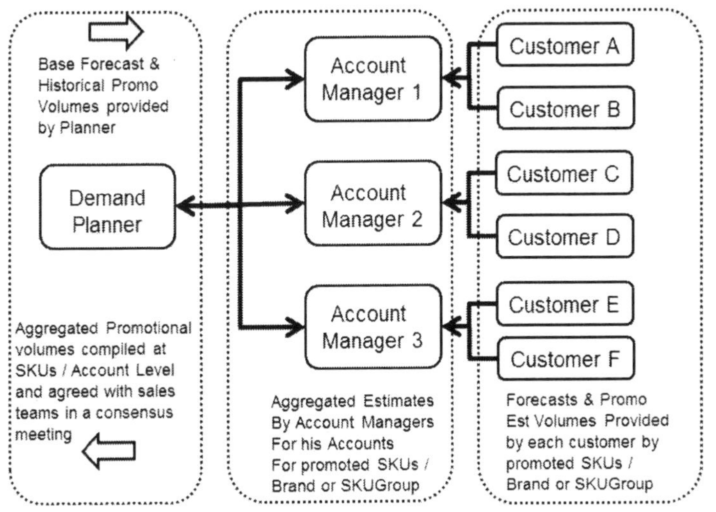

Account Level Promotions Uplift Planning Example

The planning process in this case is also dependent on how the sales teams are organized within your company. They could be organized by accounts where you have sales managers focussed on selling / servicing specific accounts (as in the case of a manufacturers sales managers selling to specific retailers), or they could be organized by categories, channels, Brands or Regions etc. There would be minor variations in all these cases with the same managers called differently and their focus being on different objectives , but from a Demand Planning perspective it will all boil down to SKU level promotions estimated volumes (either by account , region, category , Brand or any other dimension).

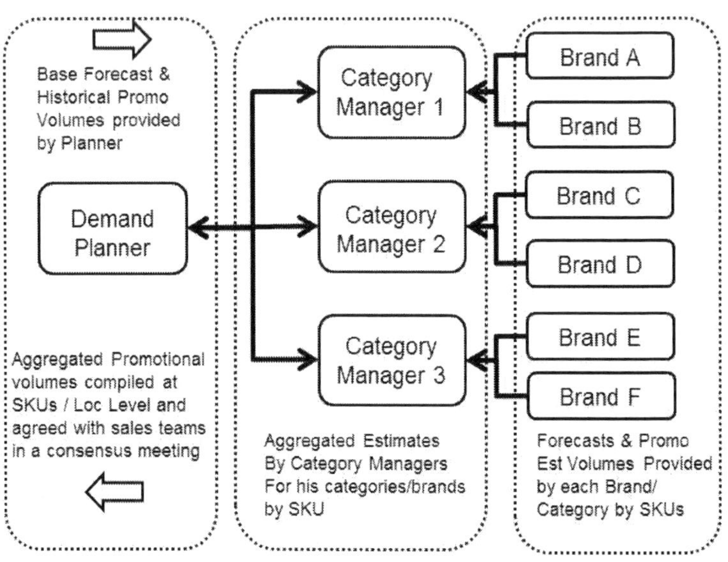

Category Level Promotions Uplift Planning Example

One area where this may not be very beneficial is New Product promotions, or products that have very short history. In most cases the estimates provided by the sales team may be overestimated due to a positive Bias towards their accounts, products or categories. In such cases the planner need to constantly challenge the forecasted uplift basis.

- **Statistically estimate promotional uplifts.** This is usually done either within your Demand Planning system or externally using statistical tool, and then loaded into your demand planning system.

A simple approach to statistically estimating promotional uplifts is given below:

Extract Prices: Price History is extracted at the SKU level for every SKU. This should cover

- Prices / Price Reductions (these are direct reductions to SKU level prices made during promotions)
- Effective Price Reductions (these are indirect changes to prices that need to be translated to reduced prices. A buy one get one free promotion will mean a 50% reduction in price)
- Identification of Historical periods which are promoted

Analyse History : This data is then used to analyse Historical Sales (either in statistical softwares, manually in excel or advanced demand planning systems which support statistical estimations of promotional uplifts) to extract Price Elasticity of Demand coefficients.

At a basic level Price Elasticity of Demand refers to how much demand changes by, for a unit change in price. For most goods sold in the market it is an inverse ratio, that is as price increases, demand decreases and vice versa. In such cases if you have historical examples of price changes, you can compute the basic price elasticity for historical promotions. This elasticity can then be applied in future , assuming that we have a Base Forecast and are aware of the price changes that we plan to make (through promotions).In the example below, a company promotes a product, which normally sells at £ 0.20 per unit. The normal average sale for the product is 40,000 units per week. When the company promotes the product at a reduced effective price of £

0.15 per unit, it generates an increased sale and sells 50,000 units per week.

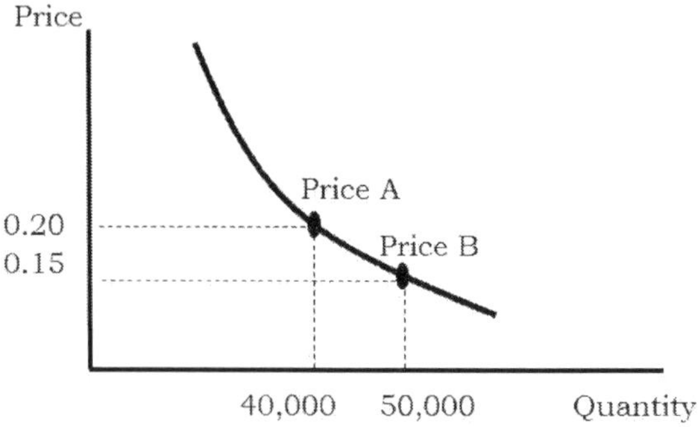

Price change impact on Demand

Note: In this example, at first glance it may seem a loss making proposition as the company actually seems to be losing money, generating £ 7'500 per week in a promoted week against £ 8,000 per week in a non-promoted week (There is of course the cost of the promotion on top as well!) . However they company may be getting Trade Allowances and sharing the costs with its suppliers, running the promotion to liquidate excess or old stock, or simply using the promotion to drive in more customers.

The Price Elasticity Coefficients may be:

- Own Elasticity Coefficients: This is the change in demand that is caused by changes in an Items own price.
- Cross Elasticity Coefficients: This is the change in demand that is caused by changes in price in other items (also called steals or cannibalization, this is discussed separately later).

Generate Base Forecast: Once the Price Elasticity of Demand has been estimated, the next step is to generate a base forecast using Cleansed History. You will recall that it is recommended that History be cleansed of all promotions impacts and outliers to generate a Base Forecast to reflect average sales during a non-promoted period. The generation of base forecast would usually be done automatically by your Demand Planning system.

Apply Price Elasticity Coefficients to Forecast : This can either be done outside your Demand Planning system and the result loaded into your Demand Planning System as promotional Uplift Forecasts, or some of the advanced Demand Planning Systems may be able to apply elasticity coefficients to the base forecast internally (sometimes even calculate the elasticity coefficients themselves).
The application of the elasticity should generate an estimated uplift on top of the base forecast based on the effective price change expected in the future. This assumes that the planner is aware of the future periods in which a future promotion is to happen, as well as the effective price change that is planned as a promotional offer.
In most cases this estimated promotions uplift computed statistically, is then reviewed by the sales teams and may them be modified or overridden.

Key points related to statistically estimating promotions uplifts: Statistically estimating uplifts can be done in the following cases:

- Pricing and Promotions history is available.
- Product has been promoted in the past.
- Product is not on continuous promotion (for example some product may be on promotions all year long, in which case they are not real promotions).
- Product has a relatively stable base forecast (not too spiky).
- Product average volume is not too low (as elasticity has a multiplier effect).
- Price coefficients are relatively stable and don't need to be created every week. In fact for stable products you could do this once or twice a year.
- Price coefficient calculations and application in future need to factor in the natural seasonality of a product.

An approach to generating automatic promotions uplifts

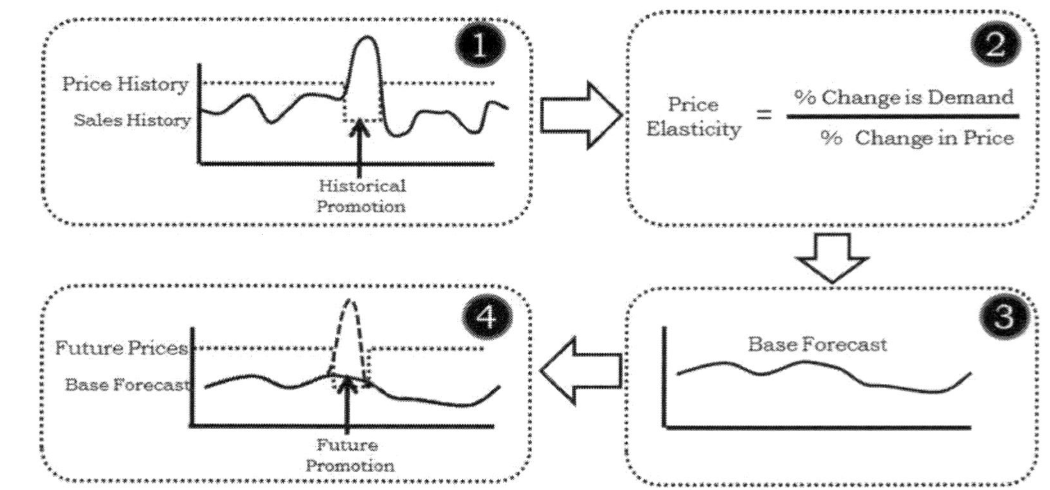

Step1: Load and extract prices for Historical Promoted periods.
Both Direct and Indirect price reductions need to extracted at Item level.

Step 2: Analyse SKU History and compute Price Elasticity of Demand of Item.
Exclude New Products or Products that have never been promoted.

Step 3: Generate Base Forecast from using Cleansed History (i.e History where promotional peaks have been removed).

Step 4: Generate expected Promotions uplift for future promotions by applying the Items price elasticity to the Base Forecast for the future promoted period.

Steals or Cannibalization Effect

Steals or Cannibalization is a term for the reduction in Demand for a product because the Demand is moved to another product that may have been promoted (or a new product launched). For example in case of a company , if there is a promotion across a Drink A , there may be a corresponding reduction in sales in that period for other brands of drinks (Drink B and Drink C etc) because a customer that would have purchased Drink B and Drink C buys Drink A instead.

Cannibalization is usually expected to have a short term impact limited to the duration of the promotion. It's expected that as soon as the promotion is over most customers will revert back to their original preferences. Sometimes the steals impact may be permanent and may be unanticipated. For example a manufacturing company may launch a new product and suddenly find that demand for an existing product is being Cannibalized by the new product. There may also be cases where a company deliberately launches new products to cannibalize demand from existing products that are planned to be phased out or products which are expected to be cannibalized by new products from the competitors.

> Note: Steals is a term usually used by Retailers while Cannibalization is preferred by most manufacturers.
> Both can be used interchangeably.

Cannibalization may also occur for the same product across time or across different channels. For example an online promotion may steal volumes away from physical stores for the same product.

It's also important to note that not all promotions have a Cannibalization impact. These are usually promotions which don't result in a price incentive (for example packaging changes, positioning of products, specific product flyers) or are mainly to increase consumer knowledge and awareness.

The Demand Planner is expected to understand the Cannibalization Map (or Steals relationships) between promoted and non-promoted products. In most companies he will also be expected to manually reduce demand for the non-promoted products whenever a cannibalizing product is promoted.

Key Manual steps that a planner will usually need to execute are:

- **Identify Cannibalization Relationships**: The first step is for the planner to analyse history and develop a good understanding of the companies promoted products. He needs to engage in a joint exercise with the Sales and Marketing Teams to arrive at an initial set of products that are expected to cannibalize Demand from each other when they are promoted.

- **Compute Cannibalization Strength:** Once the initial set of Cannibalization relationships is drafted, the planner can then compare History of the promoted products with History of the Non-promoted products to identify products which display negative correlation during promotions. A negative demand correlation means that when the demand for one product increases, the demand for the other decreases and vice versa. The products which reflect the strongest negative correlations are the ones where the planner needs to focus, to reduce the Demand of the non-promoted products (as the smaller correlations will have minimal impact on Demand and may just increase planner workload).As part of this step the planner may need to compute cross-price elasticity and take the product seasonality into account.

  This exercise (sometimes done using analytics or excel based toolkits) should give the planner a set of Cannibalization products for every promoted product where the relationship should remain the same in the medium term (i.e. you don't need to do this exercise frequently, once or twice a year should be enough).

- **Assign New Products:** As soon a new product comes in and is setup in Masterdata and demand planning systems, the planner has to ensure it is added to the Steals or Cannibalization map. Since a new product does not have history to enable calculation of cannibalization strength or cross price elasticity of its own. The planner has the following options to model cannibalization for new products:
    - Manually
    - Assign from aggregated level
    - Assign from like product
    - Assign from product being replaced by new product

- **Apply Cannibalization Impact**: Once the initial set of steals relationship is drafted, the Cannibalization Impact should be computed automatically by most demand planning systems for any future promoted periods. The volume reduced is usually modelled as a percentage or factor of the net forecast of the non-promoted product that is cannibalized (and not a percentage of the uplift volume for the promoted product). This is done to ensure that the total cannibalization impact is not greater than the total forecasted volume of the cannibalized product.

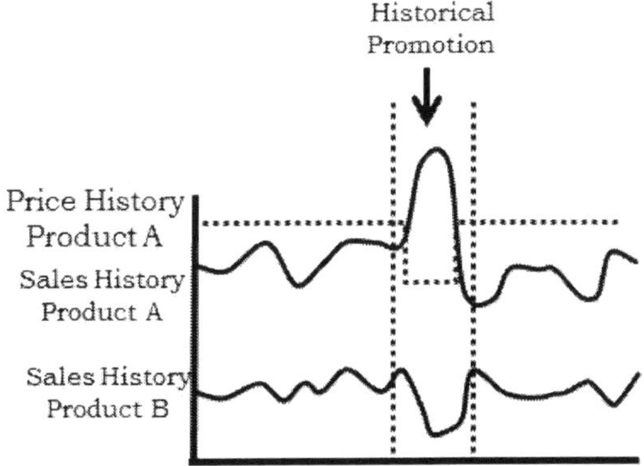

Demand for Product B goes down when Product A is promoted

In some cases the Planner may have to compute the demand to be reduced for the Non-Promoted product, during a future promotion on the promoted product. This can be done in two ways.

- Manually estimate the cannibalization volumes (with the Sales Team's inputs). This is usually an exercise based on historical volume reduction observed for similar promotions. This assumes that your company maintains historical records of promotions. This is also manually intensive and subject to Planner and Sales Force Bias.
- Use the Cross price elasticity Coefficients of Demand for the non-promoted products to forecast the reduced volumes (in an external tool/excel) and apply/load the cannibalization impact volumes generated.

$$\text{Cross Price Elasticity} = \frac{\text{\%age change in demand of Non-Promoted Product}}{\text{\%age change in price of Promoted Product}}$$

- **Review and Approve Cannibalization Impact**: Once the cannibalization volume impact is estimated by the Demand Planning team, the Marketing and Commercial teams will use the estimated reduction in volumes within their Promotions or New Product launch profitability analysis. A strategic decision is then made to either go ahead with the Promotion/New product Launch or the volume estimates are revised and reapplied. The Demand Planner needs to be actively involved in these discussions to understand the basis of the volume changes requested.

- **Quarterly Review and Fine-tuning of cannibalization Map**: On a quarterly basis the Demand Planner should review the setup of the Cannibalization Maps to review if any products need to be excluded or included. New Products launched may need their cannibalization Maps adjusted and the coefficients' / strengths of cannibalization may need to be re-evaluated based on the most recent history.

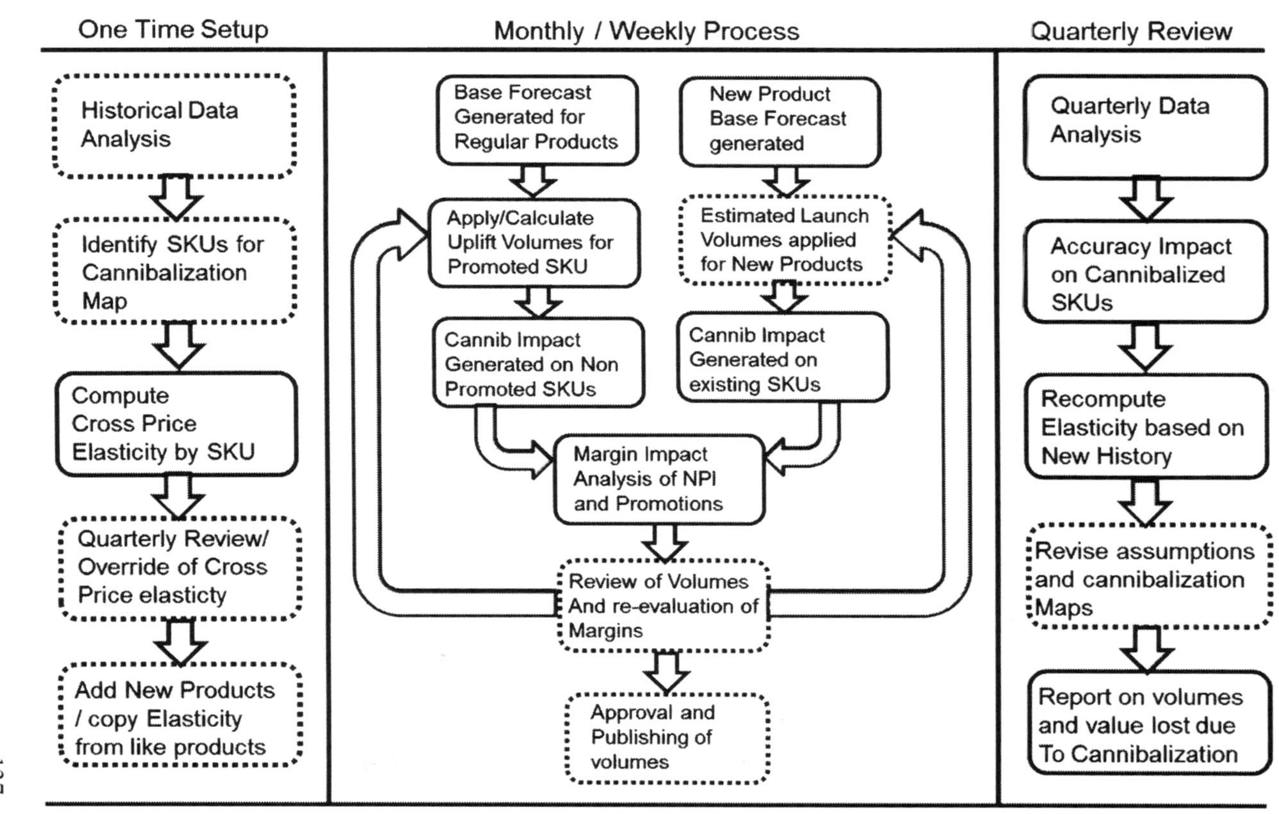

Example Cannibalization Framework /Process
One Time Setup
Monthly / Weekly Process
Quarterly Review
Historical Data Analysis
Identify SKUs for Cannibalization Map
Compute Cross Price Elasticity by SKU
Quarterly Review/ Override of Cross Price elasticty
Add New Products / copy Elasticity from like products
Base Forecast Generated for Regular Products
New Product Base Forecast generated
Apply/Calculate Uplift Volumes for Promoted SKU
Estimated Launch Volumes applied for New Products
Cannib Impact Generated on Non Promoted SKUs
Cannib Impact Generated on existing SKUs
Margin Impact Analysis of NPI and Promotions
Review of Volumes And re-evaluation of Margins
Approval and Publishing of volumes
Quarterly Data Analysis
Accuracy Impact on Cannibalized SKUs
Recompute Elasticity based on New History
Revise assumptions and cannibalization Maps
Report on volumes and value lost due To Cannibalization
Dotted Lines indicate Manual/Planner Activity

Simple Approach to Cannibalization

Modelling Cannibalization impacts in Demand Planning Systems is sometimes ignored or left entirely to manual input, as it is perceived to be a complicated process. A few reasons for this are:

- Many companies do not maintain/store historical data of promotions and prices. Even when they are stored, they are usually in different systems and in formats unusable or not easily integrateable with Demand Planning systems.
- Application of cannibalization and computation of coefficients at SKU level may be cumbersome due to large number of SKUs, or less number of planning resources.
- The planning systems may simply not have the capability to model/apply cannibalization.

In such cases rather than completely exclude Cannibalization, companies can make use of a simplified approach to applying cannibalization. Key elements of a simplified approach would be:

- Manual Judgement based Cannibalization.
- Application of cannibalization for key items only.
- Application for large volume impacts only.
- Application for major promotions or customers only.
- Volumes impact planning only. No Margin or revenue analysis.
- Application of cannibalization impact only in the short term horizon (where promotions volumes are expected to be frozen).

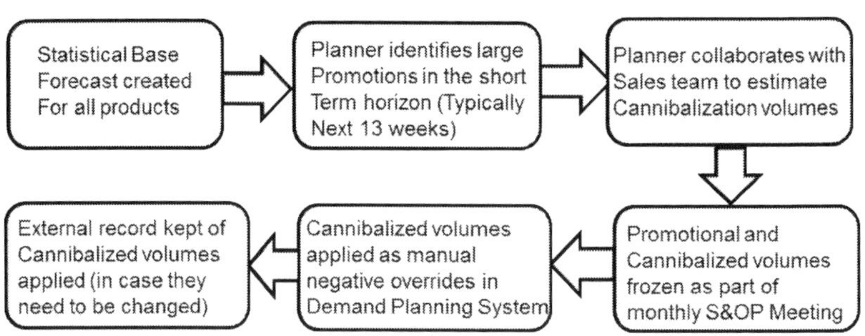

A Few notes related to Cannibalization

Aggregate level elasticity: One approach that can be used whenever a company does not have reliable granular level history is to use aggregate level elasticity coefficients as indicators to compute cannibalization at SKU level. The aggregate level may be brand, sub-brand or a custom grouping of SKUs where an average price at aggregate level makes sense. This can also be done to reduce complexity and maintenance requirements.

Lagged Cannibalization: In some cases , the customers are made aware of an upcoming promotions deal well in advance. This may be through advertisement, flyers, coupons, social media or word of mouth. This leads to a lagged cannibalization effect on other products where the customer demand for other non-promoted products drops in anticipation of the promotion. A reverse effect is observed when the promotions are not advertised and communicated to the customers. In this case customers slowly become aware of the promotion and the cannibalization impact sets in at a later stage than the start of the promotion. Modelling Lagged cannibalization needs consumer insights as well as advance information related to advertisement campaigns.

Space Cannibalization: Some products have a reduction in demand because of the size / pack-size of promoted products. This may happen because the consumer does not have enough space to store the promoted and non-promoted products in his trolley, car, house, pantry or fridge. This usually applies to products that are large in size. It is sometimes modelled into demand planning from Manufacturers to Retailers where the retailers warehousing and storage constraints are known. However, this is rarely modelled or measured by retailers as they don't have consumer specific information related to storage.

The Halo Effect

Halo Effect (also known as Product Affinity) is similar to the Cannibalization (Steals) effect in the sense that, it's the effect on Demand of a non-promoted product by another product on promotion. The difference is that in Halo effect, it's a positive effect and an increase in Demand of the non-promoted product. For example you may find that the demand of snacks or potato chips goes up when there is promotion on a soft drink or cola. This is because the two products are complementary and go together. There are many products which form a "basket" of goods from a consumer point of view, Cola and Chips, Bread and Eggs. A product may also experience a Halo Demand due to its positioning or close proximity to another popular or promoted product on a retailer's shelf.

There are a few other types of Halo Effects. The most common of these are:

Angel Halo: When a very strong brand is promoted it may lift the volumes of the whole category and associated brands.

Own Halo: In some cases (notably for new products), a strong promotion may induce more customers to test/ switch, thereby permanently lifting the future Base Demand for the new product.

Competitor Halo: In this case, demand for your product may increase due to promotions by your competitors which may be increasing the whole size of the market.

Basket Halo: This example was detailed above and happens when a product that forms a part of a complementary basket of products is promoted, lifting the volumes for the whole basket.

Halo effect is not commonly captured, but it does provide an opportunity to increase sales by correctly targeted promotions and to avoid unnecessary promotions costs on products that would have seen an increase in demand in any case (through the halo effect).The planning teams don't usually focus on Halo Effect, especially if their key focus is mainly on reducing costs and improving forecast accuracy, and not on increasing sales. It may also mean that Halo effect is not captured historically if stockout data is not correctly maintained and analysed.

The steps to applying Halo Effect are similar to the steps for Steals. The planner needs to analyse History to establish halo relationships , compute cross price elasticity using the same formula as in Steals (though the cross price elasticity will be positive in case of Halo) and then apply the Halo effect by applying the elasticity to the base forecast of the Halo Products for future promotions periods.

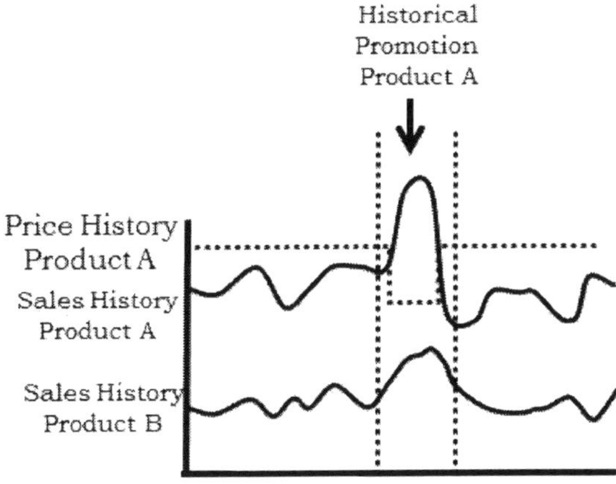

Demand for Product B goes up
when Product A is promoted

Pantry Loading

Pantry Loading is cannibalization done by the Item in one period on the demand for the same item in the next period. This happens when a product is promoted or its price reduced and the customers' stockpile the product. This usually happens for consumer products that can be stored for longer durations and that the customer buys regularly. This results in the customer not buying the product again till he has consumed his own stock level. The outcome is a sales dip immediately following the promotion before the product returns to its normal demand level.

Pantry loading, of course does not apply to all types of products. The customer cannot buy and stock milk for example or other perishable products. The customer will also not but four pair of shoes for the next four years.

The Demand Planner is expected to understand the effect of Pantry Loading and may want to include pantry loading effects while evaluating promotional effectiveness. It's also possible for the planner to analyse historical periods and evaluate the Pantry Load Dip post every promotion period, for key items. He can then modify the future forecast after every future promotion to model an equivalent dip to reflect historical patterns. This is usually done as below:

- **Manually** – reducing the post promotions forecasted Demand.
- **Using Promotions Profiles** covering the promotions as well as the post promotion period. Some advanced Demand Planning applications will allow you to create promotions profiles or patterns which define the ratio of uplifts as well as downward dips during a promotion as well as post promotion period. .

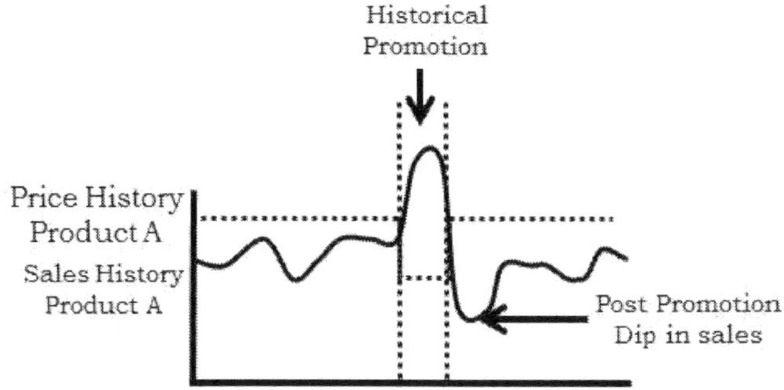

Pantry Loading Effect pulls the Demand from the week following the promotion into the promoted period

A Generic Promotions Business Process

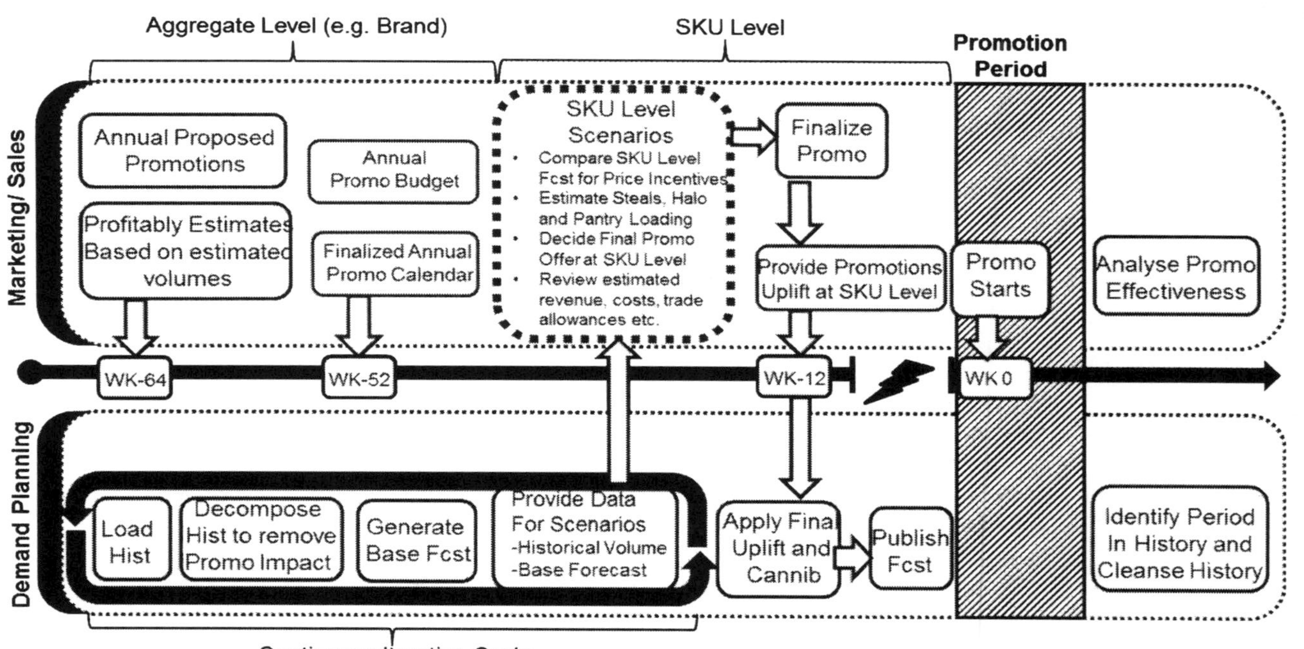

Evaluating Promotions Effectiveness

It's important for the Company to measure Promotions Effectiveness once a promotion finishes. Key points to be kept in mind are:

- Analyse at least two weeks data past the promotion end date to capture any Pantry Loading Effects
- Include Revenue effects from Steals and Halo Effect.
- Record and compare Revenue as well volume changes compared to Initial promotions estimates.
- It's important to record and analyse non-financial benefits as well.
    - Reduced Wastage of perishable products.
    - Sales of Event related special pack products (e.g. Easter).
    - Increased Consumer trial of new product.
- Measure Promotional Effectiveness at SKU level as well as aggregate promotion level. In case the promotion covers a basket of products, it's possible that some individual products have a low response to the promotion while on the whole the promotion is very successful when all the products are taken into consideration.
- Incorporate all cost (and benefit) elements that you would not have incurred if the promotion was not done.
    - Trade Allowances
    - Marketing costs
    - Inventory Holding costs for excess Inventory
    - Increased Transport
    - Damages / Returns and Wastages
    - Special Print and Packing costs
- Share learnings and information learned between all stakeholders.

Thought Points........

- [ ] In what cases would a company promote products.
Are Promotions always financially beneficial.

- [ ] How frequently can the sales team change the estimates of Promotions Uplifts.
Are there cases when the sales team cannot change the Uplifts.

- [ ] What is Price Elasticity of Demand.
What value would it be for most promoted products. Positive or Negative.

- [ ] Which of the following is beneficial to the company. Steals, Halo or Pantry Effect.
What would happen if you don't measure and adjust for Steals Effect.

notes.................

notes..................

notes...............

Chapter 9

Demand Planning Systems

Every company having a Demand Planning System or in the process of implementing a Demand Planning System needs to have a basic level of systems capability and organization of data for the Demand Planning System to work effectively. Most Demand Planning systems are dependent on data from external systems and sources and do not work as a stand-alone kit on their own. Demand Planning systems also have an impact in the areas of:

* Resources (Analysts, Maintenance , IT and Support)
* Costs (Infrastructure , Application , Support and Data)
* Flexibility (requirement to follow standard processes)
* Other systems (system compatibility)

All of the above mean that organizations have to be evolved to a sufficient level of operations, business process and organizational structure to benefit from a Demand Planning System.

The diagram below describes types of Demand Planning Approaches used by different organizations:

No Demand Planning	Manual Demand Planning	Custom Developed Systems	Best of Breed Systems
• Small Businesses or Make to Order Businesses who make specialised products to customer orders • Focus may be on operations / manufacturing capacity utilisation. • Some companies may look to external sources for forecasts or accumulated sales force inputs to generate demand plans.	• Small Businesses ,Businesses with very small number of SKUs or businesses with a fixed set of small customers. • Worksheets or paper based planning. • Simplistic smoothing or averages may be used to generate forecasts. • Demand Planning usually lies within the Sales/ Marketing function.	• Medium or large businesses running on old legacy systems. • There may also be organizations that have special requirements or business processes. • Lastly a company may want to gain a edge in Demand Planning and decide to have a custom built application rather than a application that anyone else (their competitors) can also have.	• Best of Breed Demand Planning Systems are dominated by a handful of large software companies. They provide out of the box forecasting and planning capabilities as well as customisation to a companies specific business requirements. • Mostly used by large global companies with structured systems and business processes.

A Generic High Level Systems Overview

The Systems and Software within a company allow for smooth flow of data and information to support their business processes. Most medium and large companies (especially in Retail and Manufacturing) will have some of all of the systems defined below. There are multiple companies offering software and systems for each of these areas, but we will just be covering the generic role of some of these systems and how they interact together at a high level.

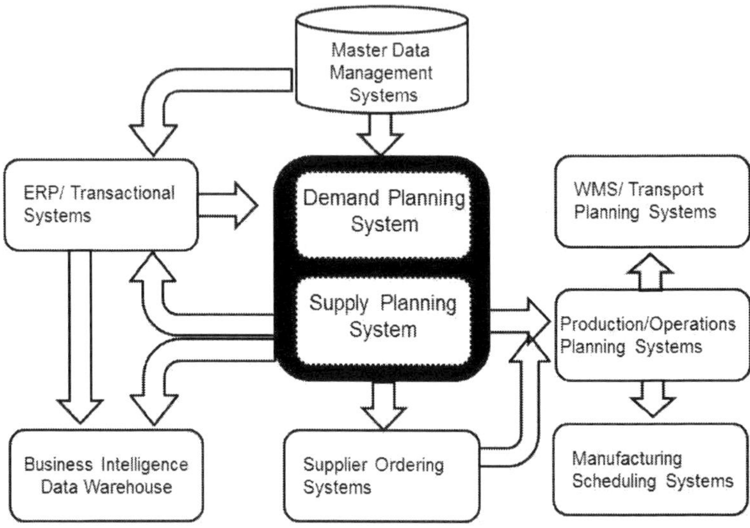

* **Master Data Management (MDM) Systems:** In an organization, Master Data is non-transactional data related to entities that interact with the organization. These may be customers, suppliers, employees, products, Product Hierarchies etc. This is relatively static setup data that does not change on a regular basis. It's essential for a company to have a single source or repository of this data to enable its different systems to talk to each other. Systems and Software that enable the company to do this are called Master Data Management Systems. These system become more critical as the company grows in size, businesses and geographical coverage. MDM provide the master data related

to Products, New Products, customers, locations, Prices and product hierarchies to the Demand Planning System.

* **ERP Systems:** ERP (or Enterprise Resource Planning) Systems hold transactional data of the organization related to Finance, Accounting, HR, Operations and other key functions. ERP Systems may be further linked to real time data sources like Point of Sales (POS) systems, RFID Data etc. ERP Systems are the source of History for Demand Planning Systems. ERP systems may also provide additional data related to Historical promotions. In most cases the data from the ERP systems will have to be aggregated or converted before it can be loaded into the Demand Planning System.
* **Demand Planning Systems:** Demand Planning Systems use history provided by the ERP systems and planner input to generate future forecasts of Base and Promoted Demand. These forecasts may be converted into different units or aggregated to higher levels within the Demand Planning system to support the planning processes. Demand Planning Systems should also use the same Master Data as used by the ERP systems.
* **Supply Planning Systems:** Supply Planning Systems use the Forecasted Demand from the Demand Planning systems, Stock On Hand from the ERP systems and customer orders imported directly to provide a future estimated position of supply requirements and projected stock positions. Supply Planning Systems may generate constrained plans (taking into account all the supply side constraints) or unconstrained plans.
* **Production Planning Systems:** Production Planning Systems are mostly applicable to manufacturing companies. These systems use the constrained supply plans from the supply planning systems and create production plans (quarterly /monthly or weekly), keeping in mind the production constrains and optimizing production to minimize costs (changeover costs, manufacturing costs, resource costs and inventory costs). Some of the advanced Production Planning Systems may incorporate Linear Programing for optimization and sequencing of production

processes and batches. The output of the Production Planning Systems would be production plans at the Manufacturing SKU level, which may be different (different aggregation, units etc) from the SKU levels at which Demand and Supply planning is done.

* **Supplier Ordering Systems:** Retailers and some other organizations that do not have a manufacturing function may use Supplier Ordering Systems to order the desired stocks against the Supply Plans generated by the Supply Planning Systems. The Supplier Ordering systems will then aggregate the Supply requirements into batches, prioritise and then release the future orders for the suppliers to fulfil. The Supplier ordering systems may also accept confirmation of incoming stocks from Suppliers and pass this information back to the Supply Planning Systems or to the production planning systems (for example ,in case the supplier orders are for parts and the assembly and some manufacturing is done by the organization)
* **Warehouse Management Systems:** Warehouse management systems control the movement and storage of materials within a warehouse and process the associated transactions, including shipping, receiving, put away and picking. The Warehouse Management Systems accept inputs data in the form of goods received from suppliers from the Supplier Ordering Systems or Receipts from Manufacturing. They generate output in terms of customer shipment schedules, pick, pack and transport instructions based on deployment plans from the supply planning systems.
* **Manufacturing Scheduling Systems:** Manufacturing scheduling systems are applicable to manufacturing companies and help plan, prioritise and sequence hourly/ daily production in such a way that resource utilization and costs are minimized. These systems will accept production and manufacturing plans at a daily/weekly level from the production planning systems and break it down to hourly/daily (sometimes by minutes) production schedules. These schedules are then utilized by the factory workers to operate plant and machinery.

Demand Sensing Systems

> **Note:** Demand Sensing is a recent term and is also known as 'Flowcasting' among the supply chain community

Demand Planning systems are mostly based on time series techniques which create a Forecast based on History. Globally most companies plan in weekly or monthly time buckets within their Demand Planning systems and use their supply and replenishment planning systems to break the future demand down to operational level (Days/ Hrs.) .However using past sales generates approximations which may or may not be aligned to the very Short Term Demand in the near future. Demand Planning systems are also slow to respond to events and changes within the weekly duration as they do not have visibility of real time or daily changes to demand signals.

A new range of supply chain solution called Demand sensing systems have recently appeared which focus on improving the very short term forecast at the SKU level based on real time / daily data to improve forecast accuracy and generate a more granular forecast for better operational and stock placement decisions.

Demand Sensing solutions typically sit on top of a company's Demand Planning solution and fine tune the weekly forecast generated by the Demand Planning Solution into a Daily SKU Level Forecast. These solutions can also accept other multiple data streams from end customers or internal partners.

Shipment history serves as an indicator of the past. This is used by the demand sensing system to develop a model of the past sales pattern. The system uses this information to break down the input forecast into daily level forecast.

Open customer orders serve as the indicator of present market activities. This is one of the main inputs for the system which helps it sense the sales rate of a SKU, and use that information to adjust the daily level forecast generated by the demand sensing system.

Demand Sensing imports fresh daily demand data, immediately senses demand signal changes compared to a detailed statistical demand pattern, and analyses partial period actual demand to perform automatic short term forecast adjustment.

Key benefits of a Demand Sensing System are:

* Daily, SKU Level forecasts with High accuracy
* Inventory Optimization and Redeployment in short term
* Short Term Forecast Accuracy improvement
* Faster Response to Demand Signals and Market changes
* Better interface between the Demand Plan and Operation plans
* Increased visibility to customer demand in the Short Term

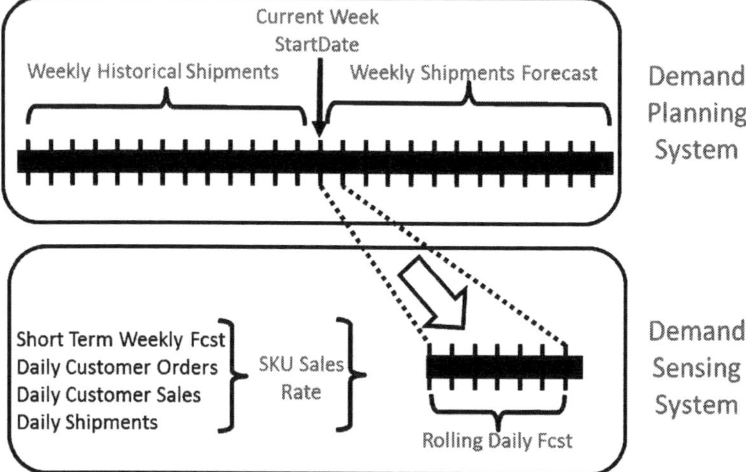

Most companies engage in Demand Sensing even if they don't use a Demand Sensing system for it. They may not realize it, but the planners engage in Demand Sensing and manually resolving short and immediate term forecast on a day to day basis as new information flows in daily. In many cases this may not be routed through their Demand Planning systems at all and may be a "outside the systems process" where the Demand Planners place ad hoc requests directly with supply. A good Demand Planning system will automate this and reduce the requirement for manual interventions.

A few notes related to Systems

In most cases the systems discussed above will have been implemented by the company at different times, by different teams and as separate projects , as such it's easy to make the whole interaction between systems much complex that the simplistic picture discussed in the last section. The organization needs to constantly keep the following points in mind to ensure smooth functioning of the systems.

* **Overlapping Functionalities**: Many of the systems may have overlapping functionalities. A single business process can also be spread across multiple systems. It's essential that processes are not duplicated / repeated and that the company decides which system will be used to perform the activities.
* **Multiple Systems**: Companies that grow through mergers and acquisitions or have spread across multiple countries may often find that different systems are being used to perform the business processes and there is no simple system map as described earlier. It's entirely possible that one country/business is using System X for demand planning while another business is using System Y for the same. In such cases it's essential to either consolidate all businesses/countries into a common system or have a central standards team to ensure common standards and processes across the multiple systems. In the long run supporting multiple applications for the same process will always be more costly in terms of time, resources and cost, than a single system.
* **Common Vendors**: It's common for a company to use a group of systems from the same vendor as most software vendors sell suite of products covering multiple areas. This is expected to make it easier for the applications to talk to each other, reduce overlapping functionalities, make it easier to upgrade and also generate other benefits like price discounts from the vendor. There may however be more than one vendors applications used by a company and it's then essential to ensure that all systems and applications are compatible or use similar technology.

Data Flows between Systems

Most of the systems store and maintain their data in their own individual Databases. These data may be at different levels, formats and with different attributes, and may not be easily transferable from one system to another. The challenge for the organization then is to ensure that they have a systems architecture which allows for the transfer of the right data, at the right time in the right format to each system in the whole architecture. The following decisions become critical for a company:

* **Transfer of Data**: This is usually done at night time when business activities are low. The transfer of data from one system to another is done via 'Batch Jobs'. These are sequence of instructions to Extract, Transform and Load data from one system to another. The IT/IS department will usually own this task and ensure that they follow the right sequence of data movement. The process may also throw out messages in case of exceptions or errors and the Demand Planner may receive some of these if they are related to Demand Planning Systems.
* **Staging Areas**: Sometimes it's necessary to convert data after it has been extracted from one system, but before it can be loaded into another system. There may also be a need to store intermediate data for auditing, issues resolution and archival purpose. This is done by creating a 'staging area', which is a database to hold this intermediate data. Staging Areas are not usually accessible to planners or application users and are used for systems integration purpose. They are also not part of any applications or Systems. A Company can have multiple staging areas depending on the need.
* **Security**: In some companies there may be systems holding critical data where they company may need a high level of security, tracking and auditing capability. In these cases the data transfers may be done using secure encryptions, firewalls or controlled environments. It's also common to have designated employees responsible for key data transfer.

* **Timings**: One of the critical things is to keep the systems available to the planners during their working Hours. This usually limits the time that can be used for updating and transferring data between systems to the night time. Also since the data transfers and flows need to follow a sequence and cannot all happen at the same time, a company will allot timing slots for each application to be updated. It's essential that the sequence and the timing of data flows between systems is correct and happens as per schedule to ensure that the systems are available to the planners by the time they come in the next morning.
* **Archival and Backup**: As time moves forward the company's data grows and after a while it may start affecting the speed and performance of the systems. It may also impact the run times of the nightly batch processes. A company will then have to decide on an Archival process at regular intervals (quarterly, biannually and annually are common). As part of this archival process the company may remove the oldest data beyond a cutoff point from the systems and archive the data in external storage. Of course this data can then be retrieved if required. A Backup process is similar to archival but happens more frequently (Daily or weekly). The backup is meant for immediate reversion in case an issue is found or data gets corrupted within any of the systems.
* **Deletion and Maintenance**: From time to time there may be a need to clean-up data or remove incorrect and unwanted data. This may require downtime for the system or a longer than normal runtime. It's essential that this be coordinated with all other systems, otherwise it's possible that changes made in one system impact other systems adversely.
* **Data Ownership**: With multiple systems in place covering different business processes but linked with common data, it becomes essential to put in place a central coordinating team or to define a hierarchy of responsibility. Otherwise there is a risk of issues being caused in some systems where the ownership of the source data does not lie with them at all. It's also important to have collaborative meetings to resolve issues between teams.

Evaluating a Demand Planning System

For a company which is deciding to implement a new Demand Planning System, it is critical that they evaluate the selected Demand Planning System in a structured and objective way. Its usual practice to shortlist and compare the top vendors selected against common criteria and then make an informed decision.

The functional criteria for evaluation are usually split into the areas of Demand Planning Process and Forecasting. Of course this assumes that the benefits have already been estimated and the company has already decided to go in for a Best of Breed Demand Planning System/ Tool. Different criteria from the list below may be critical to different businesses. If you already have a Demand Planning System implemented, you can still rate it based on the criteria below.

Criteria - Demand Planning Process

HISTORY MANAGEMENT

- ☐ Ability to Load multiple History data types for the same SKU.
- ☐ Ability to Copy, Merge, Split, Delete and Override History.
- ☐ Ability to Aggregate History Automatically.
- ☐ Ability to define different History start dates by SKU.
- ☐ Ability to view History (and History components) graphically.
- ☐ Ability to create profiles from previous Historical patterns.
- ☐ Ability to decompose history automatically.

PLANNING

- ☐ Ability to plan at Multiple Levels.
- ☐ Ability to plan in different time buckets.
- ☐ Ability to aggregate and synchronise Forecasts Automatically.
- ☐ Ability to generate reports to support S&OP Process.
- ☐ Ability to generate short term and long term plans separately.
- ☐ Ability to integrate external intelligence / Data and strategic management inputs to model forecasts.

NEW PRODUCT INTRODUCTION

- ☐ Ability to create Forecasts for new products using:
    - a. Pseudo History (copied from like products).
    - b. New Product Launch Profiles.
    - c. Manual Input.
    - d. Forecasting Algorithms.
- ☐ Ability to Model New Product Forecast in line with its own History generated after launch.
- ☐ Easily transition a New Product to a regular product.
- ☐ Ability to discontinue a product.
- ☐ Ability to flag and identify new products in the system.
- ☐ Ability to generate a New Product Forecast in advance of the new product launch.
- ☐ Ability to replace an existing product with a New Superseding Product.

PROMOTIONS AND EVENTS

- ☐ Ability to Load and integrate promotional uplifts from external systems.
- ☐ Visibility of promotional uplifts applied (at all levels).
- ☐ Visibility of promotional uplifts in History and Forecast.
- ☐ Ability to apply uplifts at multiple levels for the same SKU.
- ☐ Automatic filtering of low volume or redundant promotions.
- ☐ Approval process for releasing forecasted promotions uplift.
- ☐ Ability to undo / cancel promotions uplift.
- ☐ Ability to apply promotional profiles based on historical promotions performance.
- ☐ Automatic generation of Cannibalization impact on non-promoted SKUs (based on planner defined Maps).
- ☐ Automatic computation of price elasticity for promotional instruments.
- ☐ Market Response Modelling based promotional uplift computation.
- ☐ Ability to Move promotions from one period to another.

- ☐ Ability to define promotions and model their impact for a group of SKUs or at an aggregated level (Brand, Sub brand etc.).

PLANNERS DAY-IN-LIFE

- ☐ Ability to create planner specific day-in-life lists / tasks for them to follow.
- ☐ Ability for a manager to track the progress of all Demand Planners within the day.
- ☐ Unique Planner specific logins with related security permissions.
- ☐ Ability for the planner to work remotely (or while travelling).
- ☐ Ability for the planner to leave messages / comments for other planners in the application.
- ☐ Ability to apply filters and configure planner specific searches.
- ☐ Ability to copy a planners access and role definitions to another planner in the system.

REPORTING

- ☐ Easily define custom reports.
- ☐ Ability to add user specified data and comments for reports.
- ☐ Ability to extract and load data for Reports.
- ☐ Ability to specify automatic generation of reports at pre-specified intervals / frequency.
- ☐ Drilldown reports to granular levels.
- ☐ Standard reporting templates:.
  - a. Forecast Accuracy / Error at SKU/aggregated levels.
  - b. Forecast Bias.
  - c. Exceptions / incomplete setup / erroneous data.

EXCEPTION MANAGEMENT

- ☐ Automatically generate exceptions highlighting:
  - a. Incomplete setup
  - b. High Forecast errors
  - c. Trend changes

d. Incorrect model usage
e. Aborted processes

- ☐ Exceptions display in a dashboard.
- ☐ Ability to create customised exceptions.
- ☐ Escalation path definition for issues.
- ☐ Historical issues and resolution status stored.

PLANNER LEARNING

- ☐ Ability to easily navigate the Demand Planning System.
- ☐ Ability to easily create a new user and apply security.
- ☐ Ability to create user specific roles.
- ☐ Availability of online Help and Manual.
- ☐ Store output in easy to view files (for generating examples).
- ☐ Ability to display key (required) fields with hints and tips.

Criteria - Forecasting

BASIC FORECASTING

- ☐ Ability to configure multiple dimensional planning entities using Product, Location, Accounts, channels etc.
- ☐ Visibility of Base Forecast separate from other forecast types
- ☐ Ability to view Forecast (and components) graphically.
- ☐ Interactive graph for working directly using graphs.
- ☐ Ability to create and convert Forecasts is different units.
- ☐ Ability to generate Forecasts up to a specified duration (e.g. 2 years).
- ☐ Users able to generate Forecast manually without waiting for nightly batches.
- ☐ Ability to generate Forecasts at different Aggregated Levels.
- ☐ Ability to add user defines columns and flags to manage the Demand Planning Business Process.

FORECASTING ALGORITHMS

- ☐ Ability to use multiple Forecasting Algorithms.

- ☐ Ability to view and tune Forecast components (Trend, Seasonality and Mean).
- ☐ Ability to manage seasonal profiles and attach them to specific SKUs to model future demand patterns.
- ☐ Ability to use multiple history steams to generate Forecast.
- ☐ Ability to generate forecast in Daily, Weekly, Monthly or user defined time buckets.
- ☐ Ability to automatically recommend best fit algorithm parameters.
- ☐ Ability to model additional causal factors.
- ☐ Ability to model stepped changes in Trend.
- ☐ Ability to switch off seasonality for products with no seasonal pattern.
- ☐ Ability to automatically identify and exclude outliers from history.
- ☐ Ability to import or create Manual forecasts.
- ☐ Ability to define Parameters at SKU or Planning Component level.

COLLABORATIVE FORECASTING

- ☐ Ability to share Forecasts (and subsets) with collaborative partners.
- ☐ Ability to store multiple versions of the Forecast.
- ☐ Ability to audit changes made to Forecasts.
- ☐ Ability to undo changes made to Forecasts.
- ☐ Ability to import external Forecasts.
- ☐ Ability to approve and publish forecast for specific SKU sets.

FORECASTING SCENARIOS

- ☐ Ability to Aggregate Forecast (Forecast components) to multiple levels.
- ☐ Ability to Reconcile Forecasts using:
    a. Historical Ratios
    b. Base Forecast ratios
    c. User specified ratios

d. Equal split

- ☐ Ability to aggregate and reconcile Forecasts for specified durations.
- ☐ Ability to approve and lock changes from further changes.
- ☐ Ability to rollover unmet demand to following periods.
- ☐ Ability to reconcile Forecasts against annual sales targets.
- ☐ Ability to re-generate forecasts manually for specified SKU subsets.
- ☐ Ability to perform 'What-if' scenarios and save multiple versions of forecasts for the same period.

FORECAST ANALYSIS & REPORTING

- ☐ Ability to store historical Forecast at defines intervals / Lags buckets at Forecast Component level.
- ☐ Ability to compare historical forecast with actuals to generate forecast statistics.
- ☐ Ability to query Forecast statistics.

SPECIAL CASE FORECASTS

- ☐ Forecasting for seasonal products.
- ☐ Very low volume Forecasting.
- ☐ Forecasting for sporadic selling products.
- ☐ Forecasting for short lifecycle products.
- ☐ Forecasting for volatile products.

Rating your Demand Planning System

The weightage and importance of the above points may be different for companies but as an initial assessment you can give 1 point for each point checked, and place your system in the ranges below:

00-20	None.................	Manual or no Forecasting	★
21-40	Starter..............	Partial / Standalone Forecasting	★★
41-60	Basic..................	Supporting Basic Forecasting	★★★
61-80	Robust	Supporting Business Needs	★★★★
81-100	Best of Breed.....	Providing Competitive Advantage	★★★★★

Other Criteria

Criteria	Questions
Data	• What Data does the software need. • How frequently is the Data needed. • What Level is the data needed. • What is the estimated size of database for the system.
Scalability	• Can the software support the volume of SKUs planned by your company. • Will it be able to handle any future increase in SKUs (additional products launches, business merger etc). • Is the performance of the tool affected at High Volumes.
Security	• Does the tool have planner level security. • Can you create read only logins. • Can the tool work in firewalled intranets. • Is it possible to audit changes made to the data..
Support	• What support is provided by the vendor. • What support will the company need to organize internally. • Are any user manuals and documents provided. • Does the tool have an online Help.
Supplier	• How many clients of the supplier use the tool globally. • What is the financial status of the supplier. • What is the future path of the tool in the suppliers portfolio. • What is the feedback from other users of the tool.
Cost	• What's the total cost of ownership. • Would any existing system need to be decommissioned. • Are there any hidden costs. • What is the cost of exiting from the usage of the tool.
Workload	• What will the impact on planner workload be. • Would more resources be needed. • Would specialised skills be needed. • Will the organization structure needed to be changed.
Process	• Are any key business processes not supported by the tool. • Would the business process have to be changed. • Does the tool come with recommended best practices. • Does the tool support your industry specific processes.
Infrastructure	• Does the tool need additional investment in infrastructure. • Will the tool be Hosted or locally installed. • Who will be responsible for the installation. • Will the planners need new hardware.
Compatibility	• Will the software be used by itself, or with other existing supply chain or planning systems. • Is the software compatible with existing legacy systems. • Does the tool use technology supported by your company.

Thought Points....... .

- [ ] How do Demand Planning systems depend on ERP systems. What systems are dependent on Demand Planning Systems for input.

- [ ] How are Demand Sensing Systems different from Demand Planning Systems.
What is the time horizon for a Demand Sensing System.

- [ ] What are Staging Areas and how are they used.
Why is the sequence of Data Flows between systems critical to an organization.

- [ ] What are the Key criteria for the selection of a Demand Planning System.
What options does a company have if its Demand Planning System does not cover all critical requirements.

notes..................

notes..................

notes.................

Chapter 10

S&OP and Demand Planning

Sales and Operations Planning (S&OP) is a collaborative process through which a company continually achieves focus and alignment between all its functions in an optimal way.

The S&OP process is a communications and decision making process that sets the direction, priorities and the boundaries for the rest of the organization. It regularly and routinely reviews customer demand and supply resources and "re-plans" quantitatively and qualitatively across an agreed upon planning horizon. The re-planning process occurs at least monthly. Implemented correctly the process focuses on change from the previously agreed upon Sales and Operations Plan. The process helps the management team understand the current level of a company's performance vs its plan. How did the company achieve its current level of performance, and what can be done to improve future performance. S&OP is primarily focused on future actions and plans keeping in mind various constraints faced by all functions in the company.

S&OP:

* Balances Demand with Supply constraints
* Gives all functions an opportunity to discuss and understand each other's constraints.
* Aligns the strategic and financial plans with changes happening at the operational level.

The output of the S&OP process is a consensus on one set of operating numbers which the members of the executive team hold themselves accountable to execute. The output includes an updated sales plan, production plan, inventory levels, new product development plan, and any changes required to the strategic plan.

The Demand Plan is a Key Input within the S&OP Process.

Sample S&OP Framework in a Manufacturing Company

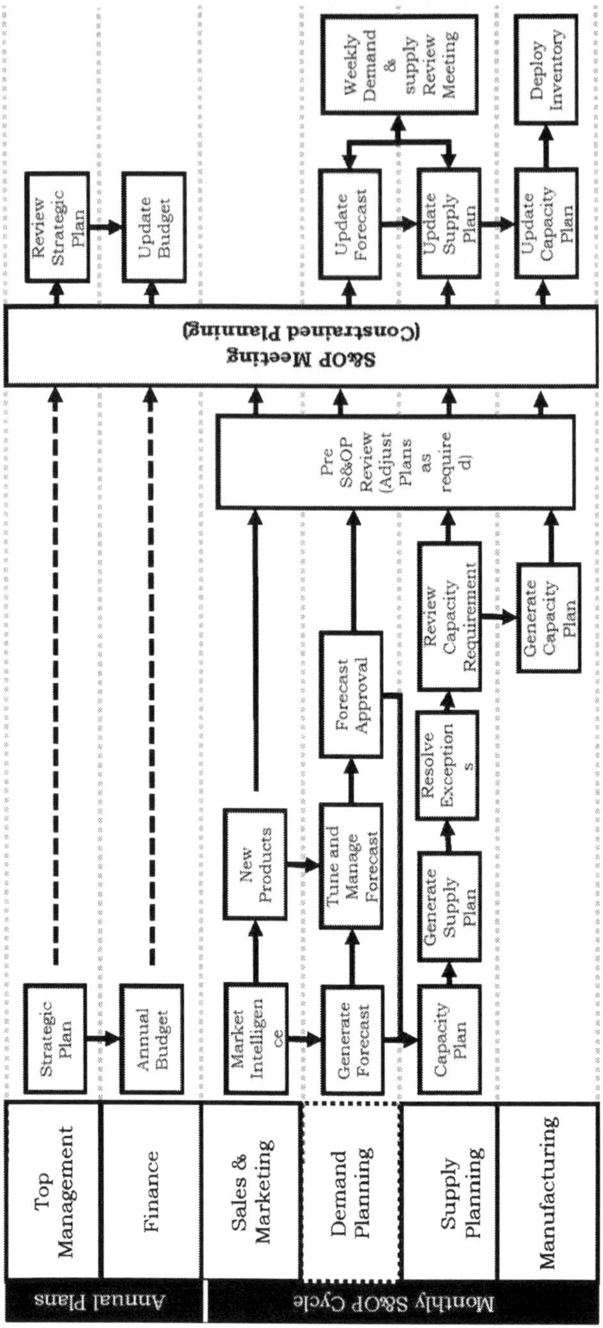

Brief Overview of the S&OP Process

The S&OP process aims to facilitate agreement between sales and operations about market opportunities and supply possibilities and agree actions to maximise sales and use of assets.

This process usually includes the following topics:
* Review of past performance, issues etc. and key learnings
* Discussions on market development and capacity situation
* Decisions on capacity development and adjustment
* Introduction of new products and big promotions

A successful S&OP Framework will usually have the following characteristics:
* Top Management ownership of the S&OP process- This is a must.
* Highest level of stakeholder involvement from all functions
* Usage of a Best of Breed Demand Planning System.
* One view of Demand Planning numbers
* Planning horizon- Usually from a month up to 18 months in the future (sometimes 24 months for products with long lead times)
* Planning data aggregated at Category/sub-category level for Retail, product family level for manufacturing companies.
* Exceptions, New Products and Promotions data may be at SKU level if required.
* Ensure visibility of the changes and agree to the change implications by all parties concerned
* Ensure that changes are achievable and support the needs of the market

Note: The Demand Planning System plays a key role in providing a single set of data to guide the S&OP Process, and the S&OP Process ensures that the benefits of better demand planning are translated to all other planning areas in the organization

A standard Framework of the S&OP process constitutes of multiple steps centred on a series of meetings .The process starts with a series of pre-S&OP meetings which are separate from the Day-in-Life of a Demand Planner (and other stakeholders). The demand planner gathers and aggregates statistical forecasts, promotional plans and effects of other events to show the most realistic future sales plans based on unconstrained demand. This data at this stage will be at the Demand Planning Item / SKU level.

The unconstrained sales plan is then passed on to the supply planning team on a weekly basis. In the first pre-S&OP meeting, this team analyses the unconstrained demand plans against production plans, inventory availability and capacity constraints.

Scenario analysis is then conducted to show various scenarios on how demand shortfalls can be addressed for constrained supply and capacity. The outcome of the pre-S&OP meeting includes an operations and constrained supply plan. It will also contain a future projection of inventory levels.

In the next Pre-S&OP Meeting, the financial plan is reconciled with the Operations / Constrained Supply Plan and analysed against financial goals, based on revenue and profitability targets, business goals and customer service level commitments.

The finance team will suggest demand-shaping opportunities that maximise the profitability where capacity constraints to customer demand exist through pricing, promotions, sourcing and optimizing scenarios.

The financial team will then come up with their recommendations as well as an agenda for the S&OP meeting. The data during this meeting is usually aggregated to a Product Family / class or subclass level.

During the actual S&OP meeting, which usually takes place on a monthly basis, all functional teams come together to discuss the recent performance of demand vs supply as well as the future reconciled demand and supply plans. Also discussed are opportunities, risks and areas that need most attention, highlighted by the finance team.

The Output of the S&OP meeting is a consistent set of collaborative plans for all participating stakeholders. The various stakeholders will then communicate the plans within their teams as a blueprint until the next S&OP meeting cycle.

A robust S&OP process also involves a set of consistent and standard KPI's (Key Performance Indicators) monitoring the operational progress against the published plans. KPI's such as Forecast Accuracy, Forecast Bias, Product Line Profitability, Revenue Variances and Customer Service Levels are commonly utilised.

In summary, S&OP is a set of business meetings and processes that enable a company to respond effectively to demand and supply variability. The outcome of the S&OP process is a reconciled plan that maximises financial and strategic opportunities and overall business profitability. The process aims to take place at regular intervals, e.g. on a monthly basis and typically looks at a mid to long-term planning horizon on a rolling forward basis.

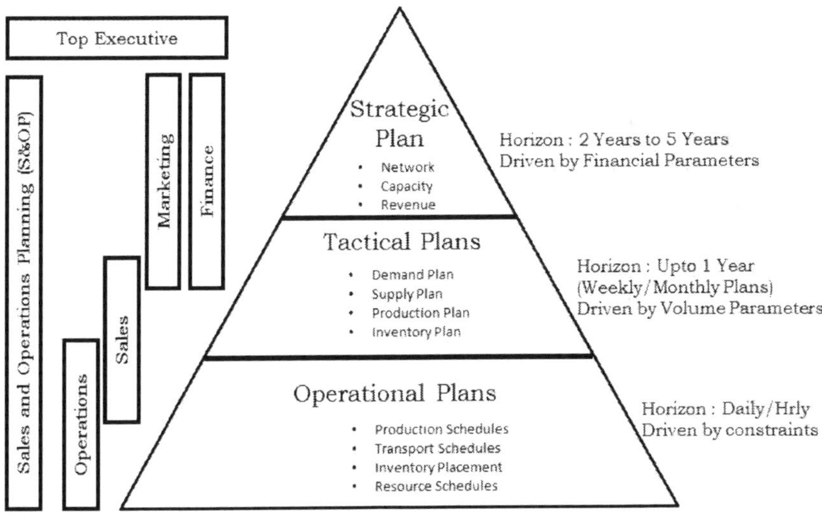

Demand Planners Role in the S&OP Process

S&OP is a Demand-Driven Process. i.e. the objective is to maximize sales while optimizing costs and respecting organizational constraints. As such the Demand Planners role is key to S&OP. The Demand Planner is the source for Demand Related information within the S&OP Framework and would be responsible for the following areas:

* **Weekly Pre-S&OP Demand and Supply Meetings**: The Demand Planner would be responsible to coordinate with Supply/Manufacturing on a weekly basis in Pre-S&OP Meetings to ensure the decisions and action points from the last S&OP meeting are properly actioned. This planning is usually at lower levels than done at the S&OP Meeting and the focus is mainly on constrained supply situations where demand cannot be met. The weekly meetings are held for course correction so that any key decisions or changes needed do not have to be kept pending for a month (till the next S&OP Meeting).

> **Note:** S&OP is also called by many other names as companies customise it to their ways of working. SIOP (Sales, Inventory and Operations Planning) , IBP (Integrated Business Planning) are just a few acronyms , but the basic concept of cross functional decision making to connect Strategic plans to Operation Plans is the key to all successful approaches.

* **Consensus Forecast**: Once the Forecast has been generated, the Demand Planner would need to perform his Day-in-life as well as all tuning and maintenance tasks. Lastly he will coordinate with Sales and Marketing to apply uplifts and Market Intelligence to reach a consensus Demand Plan. This will be done every week as new History comes in and is a must before the next task, which is the aggregation of the forecast for S&OP.

* **Aggregated Demand Data**: S&OP requires demand data to be aggregated at the product Family, Brand / Class or subclass level for the data to make sense to all stakeholders involved. In most cases the data will be needed in numbers (volume) as well as converted to cash (Value). This becomes a key monthly activity for the Demand Planner to support the S&OP Process. The Demand Planner ensures that the Aggregated Forecast has gone through the consensus process and has been reconciled with all other levels of forecast, before being taken to S&OP Meetings.

* **Review Performance Data**: Every week the Business Intelligence or Reporting teams will process data and generate KPIs related to Demand Planning. These are usually Forecast Accuracy, Bias and related measures as well as exceptions. The Demand Planners role is to review the data every week as it's generated, to ensure all the figures are correct and to investigate reasons for any anomalies. The KPIs are then used and reviewed in the S&OP meeting every month, where the Demand Planner will be expected to have answers, resolutions and suggestions for improvement.

* **Review Demand Plans in S&OP**: During the S&OP Meeting the Demand Planner would be part of the review and lead discussion around key topics impacting Demand. He would be expected to provide suggestions on improving various areas related to Demand Planning as well as have reasons for variances from the previous plans. These discussions are at Product Family/ Brand level and not the usual level that the Demand Planner works at. There may also be conversions to multiple units of measurements, value, weight, space or quantity.
* **Champion the S&OP Process in the Demand Team**: The Demand Planner needs to communicate the decisions and Action points coming out of the S&OP Meeting, within his team and the Demand Planning community. Documentation, training, workshops are all part of the scope.

* **Understand Demand to Supply Mapping**: In Most cases the Supply Plans are implemented at different levels / aggregations, than at which the forecast is generated. For example, you may be generating a forecast for a product by customer in your Demand Plans, but your supply plans may be based on an aggregated quantity for all customers. The Demand Planner needs to understand the level at which Demand Plans are used by Supply and the linkages between the Demand Plan and the Supply Plan..

* **Initiate improvement areas:** The Demand Planner will take away suggestions for improvements, as well as identify areas to improve the forecasted Demand Plans. He would make detailed designs of processes and lead any changes required to the Demand Planning Systems and Processes from a functional perspective. He would also be expected to engage in a continuous effort to improve the Forecast Accuracy, reduce Forecast Bias and share his learnings with other Demand Planning community within the organization.

* **Flag and escalate issues:** The Demand Planner is expected to identify potential issues to Demand Plans in advance and escalate them to concerned teams. This could be discrepancies in masterdata, products that could be expected to have high variability in demand due to freak weather, major events coming up or prebuild required for new products. Occasionally there may be a supply side push as the company tries to get rid of excess stock and wants to allocate additional demand to cover this.

Demand Planners Role in the S&OP Process

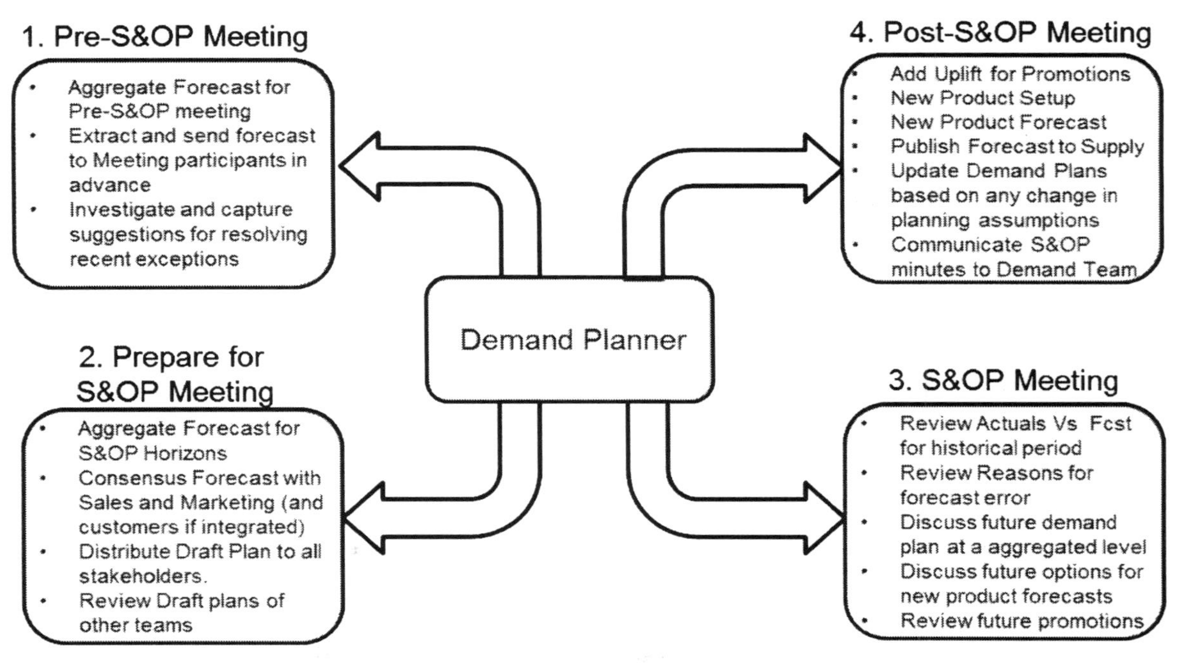

Sample Agenda for an S&OP Meeting

The following are some of the areas that may be discussed in an S&OP Meeting. It's important that the agenda be circulated well in advance and any changes or specific additions to the Agenda highlighted.

Historical Performance Analysis

- Review Last Period (Week/Month) and Year to Date
- Review Financial KPIs
- Review Forecast Accuracy at Product Family Level
- Review Forecast Bias at Product Family Level
- Review Operations Plan Accuracy at Product Family Level
- Review Cost to serve at customer account level
- Review Historical wastage and Returns

Review Planning Assumptions (included as per need)

- Review any changes to warehousing or Manufacturing capacity
- Review any changes in prices
- Review any pruning of products
- Review merger/divestment of business areas
- Review any planned changes in IT infrastructure
- Review Key manpower and resourcing issues
- Review Aggregation level changes, product Hierarchy changes etc

Forecasted Demand Plan

- Aggregated Demand Plan over 30 days,90 days and a year
- Forecasted Demand Vs Sales Targets
- GAP Analysis
- Major events and promotions forecasts
- Planned New Product launches
- Review Variance from previous projections and reasons

- Any future realignment of product portfolios
- Sales Organization Restructuring
- Major competition activity
- External Causal Factors
- Market Share growth

Future Production Plan

- Production constraints over 30 days , 90 days and a year
- Additional sourcing options
- Production Prioritisation for key products / customer accounts
- Special pack requirements
- Review Manufacturing Capacity utilization

Projected Inventory positions

- Projected cash stuck in inventory
- Projected annual inventory turns
- Safety Stocks for Major Events
- Stock Liquidations

Customer Review

- Customer Service Levels
- Key Account Orders
- Key Customer Promotions
- National Campaigns

Continuous Improvement Plans

- Update on Lean Projects in specific areas
- Update on Cost Reduction Programmes
- Update on Inventory Reduction Programmes

Implementing a Successful S&OP Framework

The more successful enterprises focus their S&OP on collaboration, profitability and continuous improvement. A successful sales and operations planning Framework will include the following four components: **people, process, technology, and metrics**.

People: It is critical to have executive-level sponsorship for a S&OP program to work. S&OP strategies fail without top-down support for the process as most stakeholders will then start bringing in their personal agenda. It's also important to create cross-functional teams that consist of sales, operations, finance and supply chain planning functions. Some companies even involve other collaborative partners and even supplier representatives. Of course in case a new S&OP Framework is being instituted, you may decide to take a phased approach to bringing in all the stakeholders. This eliminates the organizational silos and promotes shared communication and collaboration across the enterprise.

Some additional S&OP conditions that will affect the people in the organization include:

* **Training and Education**: All stakeholders and their teams need to be properly trained in the importance of S&OP and how it helps the organization as a whole.
* **Performance Measurement** :Only operational metrics approved by the S&OP team should be used, and all parties must be trained on the actions to take as business intelligence is delivered
* **Adherence to Process**: All departments and business units must follow the formal S&OP system and the Business/Department heads should be held accountable for the success of the program.

Process: Effective S&OP involves more than just holding formal weekly and monthly meetings. It is also about having visibility into demand and supply and making sure that business intelligence is continuously monitored at a executive level, and strategic plans are aligned with operational constraints. To ensure this alignment, the formal meetings should begin with the CEO (or general manager) setting the tone for the meeting by bringing up any special, driving themes or situations that require priority attention. All key functional areas of the business must be represented in the S&OP process, and a logical progression through the business must be made, including:

* Reviewing consolidated demand for all product families.
* Achieving consensus on the demand-side of the business.
* Testing the effect of plans on key constraints.
* Making adjustments to ensure optimal profit and achievement of strategic goals.
* Gauging the effects of new product introductions.
* Reviewing other special projects.
* Documenting all decisions and actions to date since the last meeting.
* Discussing possible process improvement.

Technology: Technology upgrades and advancement are also necessary parts of success.

For example, we see many companies relying on spreadsheets for S&OP. The result: siloed, inaccurate data; nonrepeatable outputs and outcomes from period to period; and an inability to scale up or down as the business changes. Further, we see results that don't provide a comprehensive view across all areas including procurement, manufacturing, sales, operations, marketing, and finance. We've also noticed that a growing number of companies are finding that their current business processes and supporting systems for enterprise resource planning, supply chain management, planning, and budgeting don't deliver what they need to keep ahead of the competition and customer demand. It's important to utilize technology enablers by developing and implementing a strategy that leverages transaction, decision-support, and business-intelligence capabilities in a real-time environment.

Metrics: You cannot improve what you cannot measure. Even companies with very informal S&OP practices must measure performance. Historically, metrics have been specific to a single function (such as sales forecasting accuracy) and involve volumetric types of measurement (such as actual vs. planned sales volumes). The emerging best metrics, such as gross margin, encompass the two-way impact of demand and supply decisions, rather than having separate and unrelated metrics for each.

Business intelligence systems today can give decision makers an accurate picture based on pre-defined key performance indicators (KPIs). These KPIs may be related to processes, product and customer profitability, order fill rates, customer satisfaction or retention, sales per employee, percent volume growth, and gross margins. The metrics can all be delivered through web-based portals and executive S&OP dashboards. For an S&OP program to succeed over the long term, companies must consider how performance measurement itself must change. This may mean putting new metrics into place as business conditions change.

Implementation: In the implementation of Sales and Operations Planning, the first step is usually the alignment of Demand with Supply Constraints. Once demand and supply are in balance the next step is to align the most current Sales and Operations Plan with the previously communicated Business or Financial Plan. Consequently the next decisions to be made should be around reconciling the current reality as identified in the Sales and Operations Planning process to previous financial commitments. If the previous promises cannot be fulfilled then expectations need to be changed.

After a company has progressed through the first two decision-making phases, it will begin to use the S&OP process to develop and monitor company projects or initiatives it has chosen to close the gap between strategic goals and the current reality.

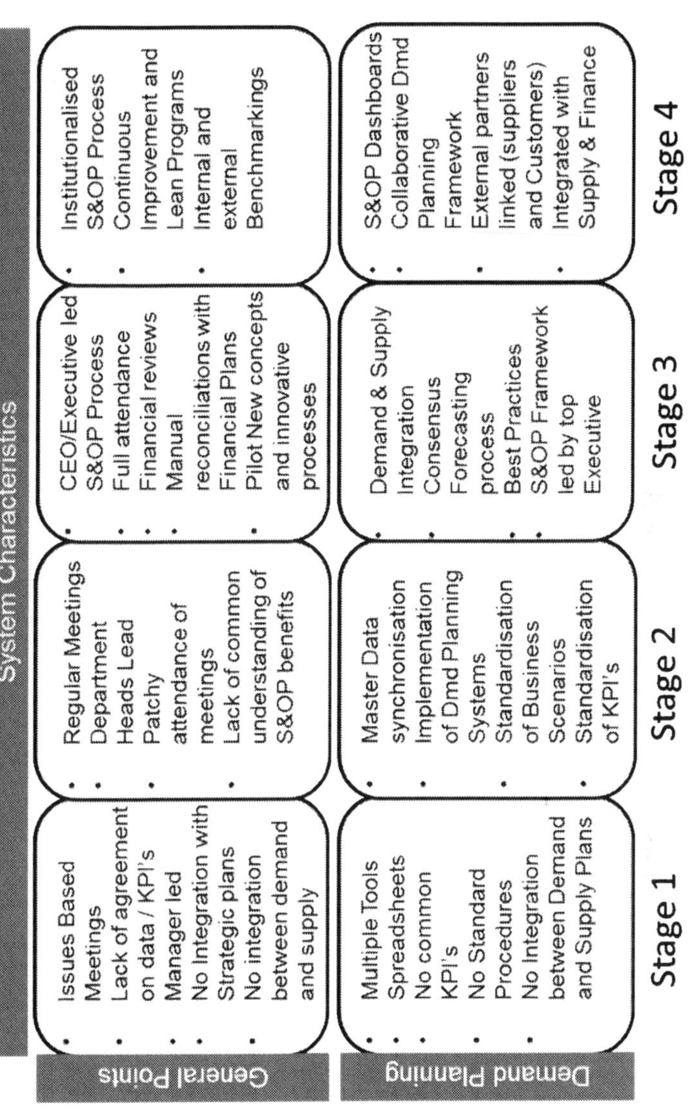
Evolution Stages of a S&OP Framework
System Characteristics
General Points
Demand Planning
Issues Based Meetings
Lack of agreement on data / KPI's
Manager led
No Integration with Strategic plans
No integration between demand and supply
Regular Meetings
Department Heads Lead
Patchy attendance of meetings
Lack of common understanding of S&OP benefits
CEO/Executive led S&OP Process
Full attendance
Financial reviews
Manual reconciliations with Financial Plans
Pilot New concepts and innovative processes
Institutionalised S&OP Process
Continuous Improvement and Lean Programs
Internal and external Benchmarkings
Multiple Tools
Spreadsheets
No common KPI's
No Standard Procedures
No Integration between Demand and Supply Plans
Master Data synchronisation
Implementation of Dmd Planning Systems
Standardisation of Business Scenarios
Standardisation of KPI's
Demand & Supply Integration
Consensus Forecasting process
Best Practices
S&OP Framework led by top Executive
S&OP Dashboards
Collaborative Dmd Planning Framework
External partners linked (suppliers and Customers)
Integrated with Supply & Finance
Stage 1
Stage 2
Stage 3
Stage 4

Thought Points........

- ☐ What are the elements of a S&OP Process.
  Is S&OP a Tool, Process or Way of working.
- ☐ Which would you implement / institute first , the S&OP Process or the Demand Planning System.
  How important is S&OP to derive the benefits of better Demand Planning.
- ☐ Why is the involvement of the Top Management critical for a succesfull S&OP process.
  What are some of the areas that may be discussed in a S&OP Meeting.
- ☐ How do Demand and Supply take mid-S&OP corrections in the weeks between two S&OP meetings.
  What can be done to resolve the gap between actual operations vs the Annual Strategic Plan.

notes..................

notes……………

Chapter 11

Demand Planning Best Practices

Demand Planning Best Practices are approaches and ways of working that have consistently shown better results of global companies and may be used as guidelines to either validate or devise processes /approaches for your company. Demand Planning is also a continuously evolving function as new concepts / software and processes are launched by experts to get better and better results in this field.

Companies worldwide are at different levels in terms of practices in Demand Planning. While some companies / industries may be quite advanced, others are still languishing in the stone ages. The following are some of the key areas where Best Practices in Demand Planning contribute to measurable and sustainable benefits.

Best Practice Area - Organization

✓ Demand Planning is located in an area within the organization where forecasting bias will be low. This is ideally a cross functional service department like supply chain or planning. The next best option is to have it owned either by Customer Service or Marketing. Ownership of the Long Term and Short Term Demand Forecasts falls within this function.

✓ The number of Demand Planners is arrived at after calculating the workload based on the number of SKUs, the business process and the Demand Planning System being used.

✓ Backup or second line of planners to assist or shadow the Key Planners. This helps in rapid transitions in case one of the planners leaves.

✓ In case of multiple businesses or countries within the organization, a central authority is deployed to govern common demand planning scenarios or best practices. The team is responsible for cross pollination of ideas between businesses as well as conducting regular workshops to ensure all the Demand Planning community with the organization is at the same level in terms of capability and knowledge.

✓ External Demand Planning experts / champions may be brought in from time to time to keep challenging the status quo.

✓ Demand Planners are business analysts, who understand the Business, the Demand Planning Processes as well as the Demand Planning System used by the company. The company undertakes internal and external training programmes to bring the skills of the Demand Planners up to the mark in case they have a gap in any of these areas.

✓ The Demand Planners are organized and aligned with the sales and marketing functions. If the company has Sales and Marketing teams by Customer Accounts, the Demand Planners should be organized accordingly. Similarly for any other organization of Sales and Marketing (by Product Categories, Regions, Businesses etc.), the Demand Planners would be organized in the same way. It is possible that one Demand

Planner is responsible for a basket of Customers/ Categories / Regions etc. if the number of SKUs planned are too less .

- ✓ Escalation structure is defined in case of issues.

Best Practice Area - Planning

- ✓ Strategic long range plan is supported by Annual sales, marketing, and operating plans.
- ✓ The business is operated using "one set of numbers" which are generated from the tactical demand planning process.
- ✓ A continuous S&OP process is followed and is championed by the highest stakeholder in the company.
- ✓ Planning Assumptions are clearly defined and revived regularly.
- ✓ Aggregated plans are converted to financial numbers for synchronising with the annual financial plans.
- ✓ Demand Plans are taken as primary input for sourcing and manufacturing plans.
- ✓ Any changes to the Strategic or Tactical plans are communicated to all stakeholders.
- ✓ Multiple level Demand Plans are created with the aggregated plans used for S&OP and for long term plans.
- ✓ Different scenarios are defined for Long Range, Medium Range and Short Term Demand Planning.
- ✓ Planner follows a predefined Day-In-Life process for routine activities.
- ✓ Standard Business Scenarios are defined and documented. Ad-Hoc scenarios may be executed by exception.
- ✓ Unconstrained Demand Planning in the initial stage with constrained Demand Planning following the S&OP Meeting.
- ✓ External Customer Forecasts and Customer Orders integrated in the Demand Planning process.

- ✓ The Demand Planning cycle is longer (or equal) to the supply planning cycle.
- ✓ All of the different levels of Demand Planning (in case of multi-level Demand Planning) are converted to a single level for supply planning purpose.

Best Practice Area - Forecasting

- ✓ The base forecast is statistical and is calculated using proven algorithms relevant to the nature of Demand of each individual SKU Planned.
- ✓ The forecast period, horizon, frequency and level of detail all correspond to the goals and methods established for the company's service levels, distribution patterns, production schedules and product management.
- ✓ The forecasted SKUs are analysed and segmented based on their demand characteristics and forecast ability.
- ✓ Forecasts are generated using forecasting algorithms suited for the demand characteristics of different types of SKUs. This usually means multiple forecasting algorithms are used within a company.
- ✓ All available information impacting Demand of products is incorporated within the forecasting algorithms. This may mean additional causal factors in addition to Demand History.
- ✓ The forecasts are analysed for error and accuracy at a SKU as well as aggregated level on a regular basis (matching the forecasting buckets).
- ✓ Minimum Planner intervention in products with good forecast accuracy.
- ✓ Minimum Planner intervention in tuning base forecasts.
- ✓ Planner's intervention for Base Forecasts is done on an exception basis.
- ✓ Exceptions are raised automatically by the Demand Planning System based on user set rules.

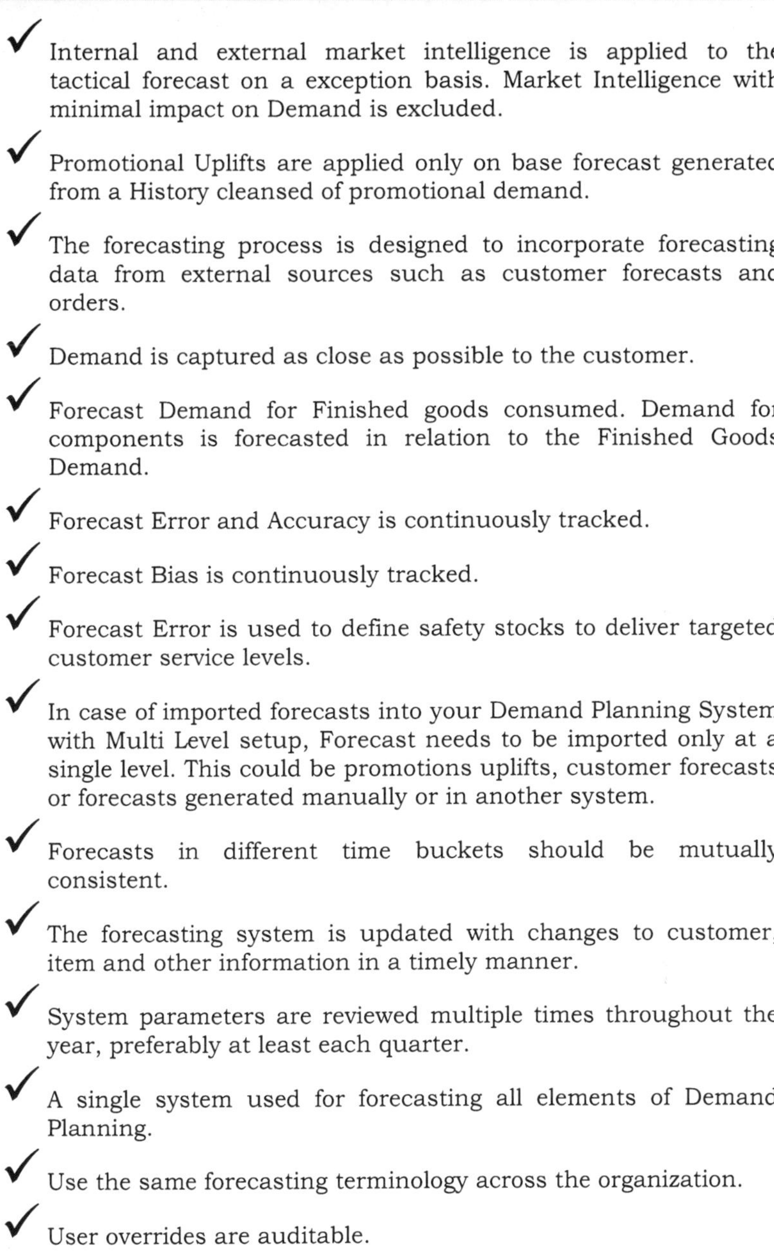

✓ Internal and external market intelligence is applied to the tactical forecast on a exception basis. Market Intelligence with minimal impact on Demand is excluded.

✓ Promotional Uplifts are applied only on base forecast generated from a History cleansed of promotional demand.

✓ The forecasting process is designed to incorporate forecasting data from external sources such as customer forecasts and orders.

✓ Demand is captured as close as possible to the customer.

✓ Forecast Demand for Finished goods consumed. Demand for components is forecasted in relation to the Finished Goods Demand.

✓ Forecast Error and Accuracy is continuously tracked.

✓ Forecast Bias is continuously tracked.

✓ Forecast Error is used to define safety stocks to deliver targeted customer service levels.

✓ In case of imported forecasts into your Demand Planning System with Multi Level setup, Forecast needs to be imported only at a single level. This could be promotions uplifts, customer forecasts or forecasts generated manually or in another system.

✓ Forecasts in different time buckets should be mutually consistent.

✓ The forecasting system is updated with changes to customer, item and other information in a timely manner.

✓ System parameters are reviewed multiple times throughout the year, preferably at least each quarter.

✓ A single system used for forecasting all elements of Demand Planning.

✓ Use the same forecasting terminology across the organization.

✓ User overrides are auditable.

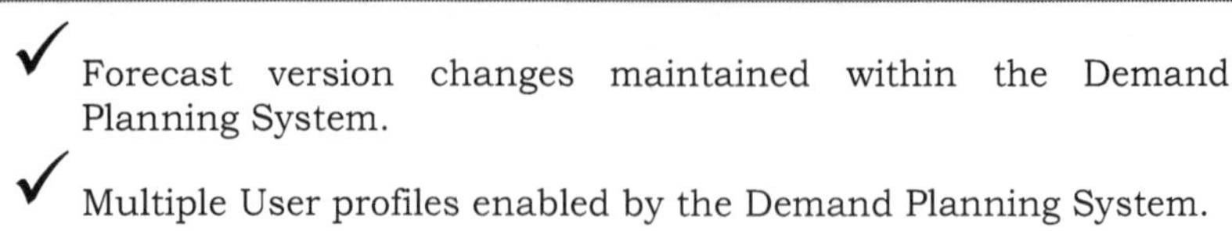

- ✓ Forecast version changes maintained within the Demand Planning System.
- ✓ Multiple User profiles enabled by the Demand Planning System.
- ✓ Forecast creation, approval and publishing enabled for user defined subsets of data.
- ✓ Planner is able to work with what-if scenarios and create Draft forecasts without publishing the forecast to other teams.
- ✓ Sales Targets can be modelled into the forecast generated by the Demand Planning System.
- ✓ Forecast can be generated using multiple models / algorithms and the system is able to recommend the best fir model.

Best Practice Area - Data

- ✓ MasterData maintained external to the Demand Planning System.
- ✓ Demand History imported from a single source.
- ✓ History imported at a single level into Demand planning system.
- ✓ History Updated at a regular frequency.
- ✓ History Filtered to exclude Negative History and Returns.
- ✓ Raw History Maintained in staging areas for the immediate short term (usually 2 weeks to a month).
- ✓ Older Historical Data removed from the Demand Planning System at regular intervals (usually quarterly or annually).
- ✓ Static Master Data (products, customers, locations etc.) is refreshed into the Demand Planning System on a Daily basis.
- ✓ History editing / update by the user is minimized.
- ✓ Use at least two years of History where available to enable seasonality to be estimated.

- ✓ A maximum of three years history used. Any history over three years will usually not add value to forecasting models.
- ✓ History is cleansed of Major events and outliers automatically by the system.
- ✓ Planner is able to define history periods to be used (and ignored) for modelling purpose.
- ✓ Standardise Static Data and File Formats (Products, Locations, Hierarchies, Data Files etc.). Alphanumeric codes used to avoid any possible issues during extraction or transfer of data
- ✓ Demand to Supply / Operations integration of Data is done based on Supply side SKUs as the drivers.
- ✓ Aggregate Data wherever it is too sparse or low volume to generate a useful forecast.
- ✓ Automate data cleansing and maintenance based on agreed rules to ensure workload is not impacted.

Best Practice Area - Promotions

- ✓ Apply promotional uplifts for only those products where the promotional impacts have been cleansed from their history.
- ✓ Apply promotional uplifts only where the uplifts are expected to be sizeable. Minor promotions or marginal uplifts should not be allowed to enhance the variability in the supply chain. They would also be covered by safety stocks in most cases.
- ✓ Model only those promotions which are expected to have an impact on Demand. Purely commercial adjustments should not be allowed to impact the Demand Plans.
- ✓ Measure Post promotional impact. The impact on demand should be measured from at least one week before the promotion starts to one week after the promotion ends.
- ✓ Promotional impacts should be measured in revenue as well units. These should include cannibalization, halo and pantry loading effects as well.

- ✓ Promotional Forecasts are readjusted using the first two days sales as leading indicators.
- ✓ Price elasticity of Demand is used to estimate the future uplifts in case of price incentives.
- ✓ Multiple promotions and pricing scenarios are evaluated to arrive at a optimized promotions decision to either maximize revenue of volume.
- ✓ Promotions Uplifts imported from external systems into the Demand Planning System are only imported at a single level in case of multi-level demand planning.
- ✓ Promotions uplift horizon is defined in which promotions uplifts are applied to the base forecast. This is a short to medium term duration (usually 12 to 16 weeks) in which the promotions uplifts are considered to be frozen and most accurate.
- ✓ Promotions uplifts for the long term forecast are applied only in exceptional cases.
- ✓ Maintain Historical record of Promotions Uplifts applied to forecasts and use it for cleansing history.

Best Practice Area – New Product Introduction

- ✓ New Product creation triggered automatically by master data changes.
- ✓ New products identified easily through the usage of flags.
- ✓ In case of a New Product superseding a existing product, the Demand Planner coordinates with the Sales and Marketing Teams to identify existing products from which history may be copied.
- ✓ Planner able to copy History or forecast from a existing to a new product.
- ✓ Planner able to attach and create new product launch profiles for manual generation of forecast.

- ✓ A process exists to transition a new product to a regular product.
- ✓ New products are indicated separately for any KPIs and Reports.
- ✓ Planners are able to generate forecast for a new product before the new product launch to support the new product planning activities by marketing.
- ✓ New Products are excluded from standard Forecast accuracy reports. A separate accuracy tracking report for New Products is maintained.
- ✓ The Demand Planning Solution is able to generate forecasts for short history products. These would be required for new products that may have come out of the new product phase but not have two years history built up.
- ✓ A collaborative approach is used for New Product Demand Planning. This would need the whole forecast to be generated by the collaborative process (including the base forecast) as the new product will not have data to generate a reasonable base forecast.
- ✓ Only short term forecast is used for the new product. Long term forecasts are based on sales targets and estimates and constantly revised.
- ✓ Track actual product consumed or bought by final customers during the new product phase.

Best Practice Area - Differentiation

- ✓ Differentiated Demand Planning rules and approaches based on segmentation of products by Average Volume and Volatility.
- ✓ New Products treated and measured separately from all other planned products.
- ✓ Planners plan demand using 80:20 rule. Focussing on Demand Plans for 20% of the products that account for 80% of the volumes.

- ✓ Demand Planning System parameters configured to automatically generate forecast for the remaining 80& of the product (and 20% volume) based on user set rules.
- ✓ Strategic and Key items handled on an exception basis.
- ✓ Review Demand segmentations on a quarterly or annual basis.

Best Practice Area - Collaboration

- ✓ Collaborate internally with Sales, Marketing and Supply.
- ✓ Collaborate Externally with Customer Accounts (in case of Manufacturers).
- ✓ Collaborate Externally with Suppliers (in case of Retailers).
- ✓ Pursue Internal Collaboration before external collaborations.
- ✓ Collaborate only on data relevant to the collaborating parties.
- ✓ Collaborate on Short Term plans.
- ✓ Collaboration on Long Term plans should be on a need basis only.
- ✓ Audit trails and versioning of forecasts is enabled to track changes made to the forecast and demand plans by multiple collaborators.
- ✓ Easy sharing of collaboration data is enabled through the web.
- ✓ Role based collaboration security to enable different collaboration parties only see relevant data.
- ✓ A strong framework of meetings , rules and business processes outside the Demand Planning and other systems supports the flow of data and changes made within the systems.

Thought Points.......

- ☐ What are the different best practice areas in Demand Planning.
  How can following best practices help your organization.
- ☐ What are some of the key Forecasting Best Practices.
  Are all Best Practices applicable to every company.
- ☐ Who could be responsible for ensuring Best Practices are followed in a company.
  How could you adopt Best Practices if you already have a different process in place.
- ☐ How would you priortise the different Best Practice areas in Demand Planning if you had to implement all of them.

notes.................

notes..................

notes..................

Chapter 12

Differentiated Demand Segmentation

One key decision faced by organizations is the approach to be taken to forecast and plan SKUs. A one size fits all approach usually does not work (unless you only have a handful of SKUs) and effort spent on improving forecasts for one SKU may not provide the same benefit as the same effort spent on another SKU. This becomes important for any company with a large number of SKUs and limited time and resources.

In this section we discuss a framework for segmenting and grouping your products for Demand Planning purposes, based on their Demand Characteristics. This allows you to apply separate Demand Planning approaches, parameters and techniques to the groups and help the planner focus his energy where he can add the most value.

It's a proactive approach where you analyse and decide your Demand Planning methodology before generating the Forecast, compared to the exception management approach where you take corrective actions after generating the forecast.

Common dimensions used for Demand segmentation are:

* Group by Demand Volatility and Average Sales Volume
* Group by Forecast Error and Average Sales Volume
* Group by Promotional Volatility and Average Sales Volume

Demand Segmentation is usually an exercise done annually or biannually outside the demand planning systems using analytics software or custom-built toolkits. The groups can then be captured /stored as a flag or parameter within the planning systems.

Grouping by Demand Volatility/ Average Volume

This approach focuses on the fact that all products have an inherent demand volatility, which affects:

* The best forecast accuracy that can be achieved for the product.
* The Forecasting models that should be used for the product.
* The amount of planner effort that should be applied to the product.

When trying to group all your SKUs into differentiated buckets, inherent volatility should be computed using common assumptions for all the SKUs:

* The level of forecasting (e.g product, category).
* What is being forecasted (e.g sales, Shipments).
* Where is the Demand captured (e.g DC, Retailer).
* The bucket of data (usually weeks as it gives better visibility on volatility).

Based on the above, the history of the products being forecasted can be analysed and placed into a four grid matrix based on their average weekly volumes and volatility. Some companies' fine tune this further into a nine grid matrix.

Note: One way to measure the volatility of a product is by computing the Coefficient of Variation for the product. This is simply the Standard Deviation divided by the mean of the product.

Don't let the mathematical terms put you off, these are standard formulas in excel and easily computed. The Mean defines the average volume that a sku is expected to sell, and the standard deviation measures how spread out the observations are from the mean (for each sku).The more spread apart the data, the higher the standard deviation. In this approach, for graphing purposes we will divide standard deviation by the Mean to give us weighted values (also known as coefficient of variation).

Steps to Generate a Basic Grouping Matrix

Step	Description
Collect one years History in weekly buckets.	Extract one years History at SKU by location Level into Excel. More History can be used if available
Filter out SKUs that cannot be modeled.	Filter out SKUs that don't have enough history (minimum 24 weeks as an indicator) or where the average values are very low or with gaps.
Compute the Mean of every SKU that remains in the data set.	Compute the mean of each of the SKUs that remain (i.e that have enough data).
Compute the Standard Deviation & Coefficient of Variation	Compute the Standard Deviation of each of the SKUs that remain (i.e that have enough data). Simple excel formula +STDEV can be used.
Determine the values for the grid bands.	Compute the Average of the mean and Average of the Standard deviation of all the SKUs with valid data. These become the x and y axis grids
Group the SKUs in the grid squares by Mean and STDEV	Group the SKUs in the four quadrants based on their Mean and STDEV.
Plot the SKUs on a Graph for visual analysis	For a visual analysis you can plot the SKUs on a scatter graph with Avg Vol on the x axis and Standard Deviation on the Y axis.

Sample Format for creating the Grouping Matrix

SKU	Location	52 Weeks Historical Actuals		A	B	C
		Week 1	Week 52	+Average( )	+STDEV( )	COVAR=B/A
SKU1001	Loc001					
SKU1002	Loc002					
SKU1003	Loc003					
SKU1004	Loc001					
SKU1005	Loc001					
SKU1006	Loc003					
SKU1007	Loc005					
SKU1008	Loc007					
SKU1009	Loc009					
SKU1010	Loc011					
SKU1014	Loc019					
SKU1015	Loc021					
SKU1016	Loc023					
SKU1017	Loc025					
SKU1009	Loc009					
SKU1010	Loc011					
SKU1014	Loc019					
SKU1015	Loc021					
SKU1016	Loc023					
SKU1017	Loc024					
SKU1009	Loc025					
SKU1021	Loc033					
			Average	X	Y	

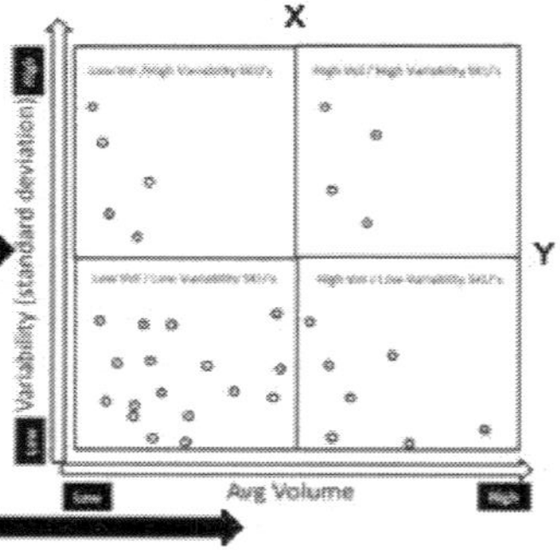

X

Y

Variability (standard deviation)

Avg Volume

Using the Differentiated Grouping Results

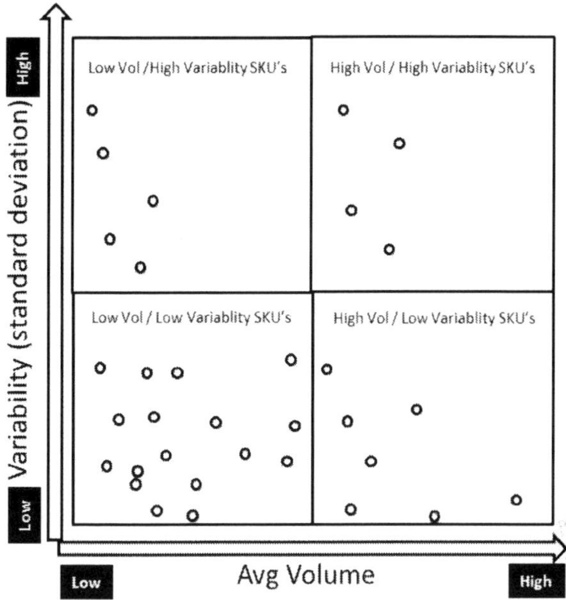

LOW VOLUME/ HIGH VARIABILITY - COLLABORATE OR PLAN BY EXCEPTION

These products usually define the long tail of low volume sporadically sold products in a company. You will usually find a large number of products in this quadrant generating a very small percentage of your total sales volume of all products. The demand for these products will be difficult to model using purely statistical models as there usually is no continuous trend, or the products may be purely seasonal. The low volumes of the products also do not justify spending a large amount of planner time modelling parameters for these products. Any of the following approaches can be taken for these products:

* **Collaborate with the Customer** : In case the demand being modelled is from a end customer or retailer, you can plan these SKUs by collaborating with the end customer or sharing forecast information for their feedback..
* **Generate a Statistical Flatline Average Forecast** : This can be further enhanced for strategically important products in this quadrant by manual input or by using causal factors to define periods with peaks vs periods where no forecast is required. Of course this will require a lot of maintenance and tuning effort and should only be done in exceptional cases.
* **Generate a Manual Forecast**: The planner may decide to upload forecast generated manually instead of using your Demand Planning System. This can be a simple copy of historical actual sales / shipments, or forecast/customer orders received from the customer for these products.
* **Use statistical models for sporadic demand**: This is the least recommended approach as all statistical models available will still require the planner to provide expected frequencies , demand levels , mean demand and whole lot of other parameters and may be no better than a simple average .

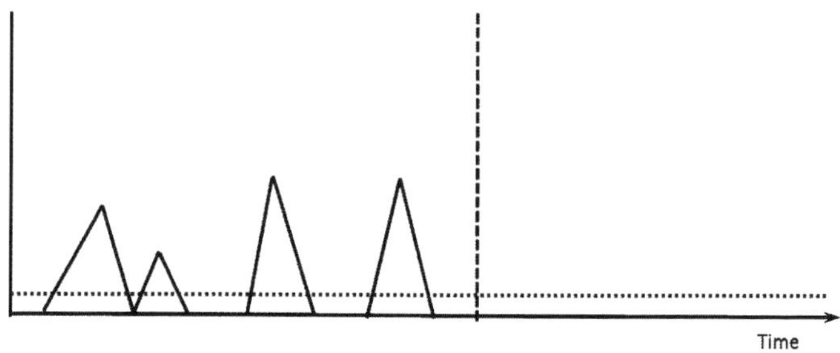

HIGH VOLUME/ HIGH VARIABILITY- PLAN UPLIFTS

These are products that have a high average base sales volume, but show high variability as the products demand reacts very highly to promotions and causes very sharp spikes in demand. This could be because new customers are encouraged to buy at the lower price point level or the product increases its market share at the cost of other products or competitors. Accurate forecasting and measuring promotions effectiveness is very important for these products. Promoting and price discounting a product which already sells high volumes can be potentially harmful if the planned demand volumes are not reached (as the company ends up discounting even the base volumes that they would have sold at higher margins).

The demand for these products will be difficult to model using purely statistical models. The following approach is recommended to forecast the products:

* **Identify products** in your Demand Planning System using flags : This should be a one time activity as the demand profiles of stable products do not usually undergo rapid changes. This can be reviewed on a quarterly or annual basis. The flags will help identify the products easily to the planners or any automated jobs / processes.
* **Cleanse history**: History for these products needs to be cleansed of the major peaks (and any major dips or stockouts) to enable the system to generate a relatively flatter base forecast. This would effectively model what the product would have sold if there were no promotions or price incentives.
* **Generate Base Forecast** from cleansed History: The base forecast is generated by the system using cleansed history.
* **Collaborate** with Sales to get a uplift forecast: The Demand planners tune the base forecast and then collaborate with the sales and marketing teams to get the planned uplifts and decision regarding future periods under promotion. This frequently needs the base forecast information as well as historical promotions information to be shared with the Sales and Marketing teams. There can also be multiple rounds of changes made to the uplift volumes based on changing promotions configurations.
* **Apply uplift**: The promotions uplift is applied on top of the base forecast. In case of Multi-Level Demand Planning, a key decision to be taken is the level at which the uplift would be applied.

* **Focus on short term horizon** : The planner focuses on the short term forecasts for planning uplifts as the promotional uplifts get frozen (usually 12 to 16 weeks). Outside this duration a forecast from uncleansed history or at a different aggregation may be used for planning purposes.
* **Manage by SKU** : This approach invariable means the Demand Planner will need to plan each and every product within this quadrant. A careful assessment of workload is recommended based on the number of products that fall in this quadrant.

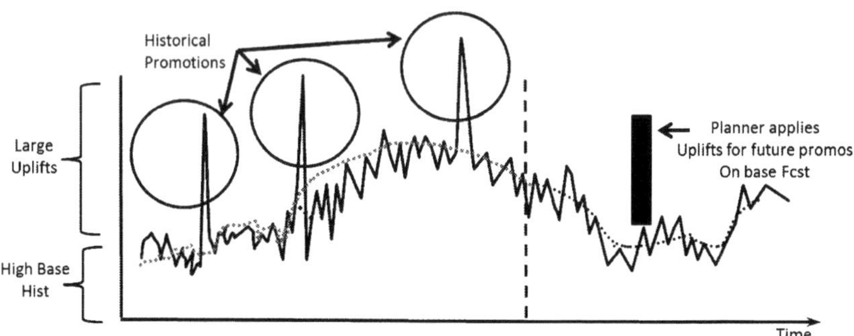

Note that these products can also be forecasted using causal factors to identify historical peak periods as well as future promoted periods. Any reasonable multiple regression model could then be expected to estimate historical peak impacts and apply the impact in the future. This approach is however, not recommended as the promotional peaks are directly related to the efforts of sales teams, price discounts offered and a host of other factors. Since these are high base volume products where a promotion can backfire if it doesn't result in sufficiently high volumes in the right periods, its recommended that a collaborative forecasting approach using sales team inputs is used (as described earlier) rather than a causal factor based approach.

LOW VOLUME/ LOW VARIABILITY – PLAN AGGREGATED LEVELS

These are products that have a low average base sales volume but have a relatively stable demand (low volatility). The demand for these is in many cases covered by the minimum safety stock settings and there isn't any great value add in trying to improve their forecast accuracy. These however need to be constantly monitored to ensure you plan accordingly if the volumes start increasing.. The following approaches can be used to forecast these products:

* Generate Forecast at an Aggregated level (Brand /Category etc) and apportion it to the individual products. This should help accumulate enough data to make any trends visible.
* Use de-seasonalized forecast or a flat line average forecast to model the average base demand.
* Set the forecast to a weighted rolling average.
* Set safety stock parameters to cover demand equal or greater than the lead time for the supply of the products.

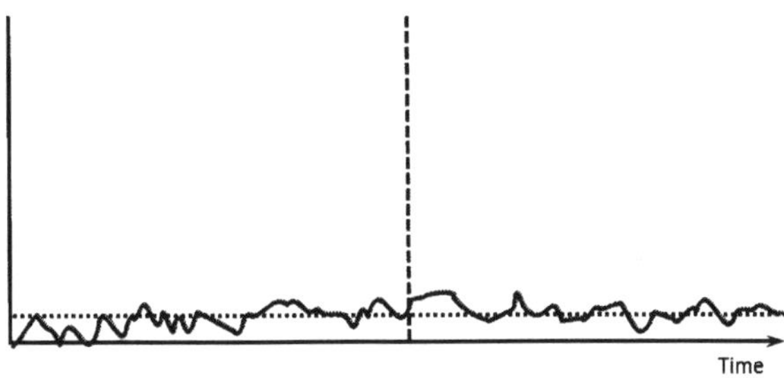

HIGH VOLUME/ LOW VARIABILITY – SYSTEM PLANNED

These are products that have a high average base sales volume, and low volatility or vairiability. These products will almost certainly not be promoted but may be on everyday low price generating high volumes. Examples of these products could be staples like Milk , Bread and eggs.As the demand is stable these products should be

forecasted using standard statistical forecasting algorithms with very less reactivity modelled in them. In fact excluding seasonality for these products usually ends up generating a better forecast.
The following approach is recommended to forecast the products:

* Forecast using standard statistical models with seasonality excluded. .
* Manage by exception in case of large forecast errors , otherwise minimise planner intervention.
* Monitor and manually manage in case any of these products start getting promoted .

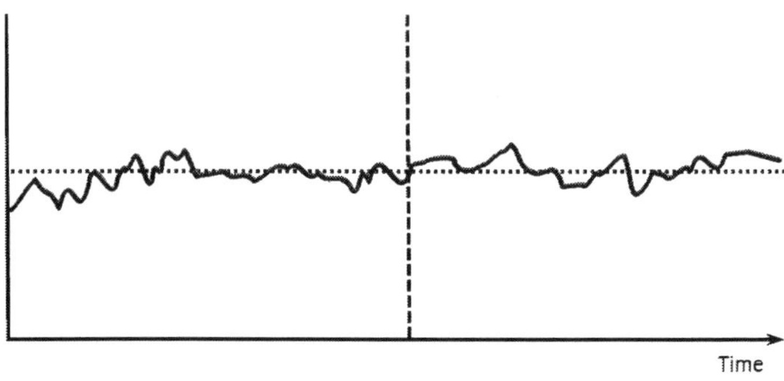

Grouping by other dimensions

Complex Grouping by other dimensions is possible but you should weigh the additional benefits of this grouping versus the additional complexity due to other data that may need to be analysed manually. Grouping by Forecast Error/Accuracy and Volume for example will need historical forecast along with actual history and may need forecast error to be managed using upper and lower thresholds. This can get very complex and is best done only if enabled by your Demand Planning solution or using a automated toolkit (there are quite a few available in the market).

Important Points on Segmentation

The key benefit of Demand Segmentation is to focus the efforts of the planner on SKUs where they can add the most value. A Demand Segmentation exercise is also very useful at the implementation stage of a Demand Planning system, to evaluate the workload that will be generated based on the number of SKUs planned.

- The Segmentation exercise needs to be done at least every quarter to monitor demand pattern changes and new products that have accumulated enough history to be modelled.

- New products and recently launched products need to be excluded.
- Sporadically sold products may be included.

- The whole segmentation exercise can be done manually outside the system and the end results stored as flags within your planning systems. The planners can then tune the parameters and manage forecasts by using these flags.

- Some systems currently available in the market simulate the whole exercise automatically within the system and enable the algorithm and parameters to be set automatically.

- The groups generated for Demand Segmentation can be further used on the supply side to manage Inventory Policy and Planning Parameters for Safety Stock.

- Lastly we need to keep in mind that there will always be exception SKUs that may need to be planned differently due to their strategic importance , profitability or criticality to the customer.

Thought Points…….

- ☐ How would you use Demand Segmentation within your company.

- ☐ Does Demand Segmentation impact other teams. Do you see any reason of the segmentation being used on the supply side?

- ☐ What do you think should be done for SKUs that don't have enough data for Demand Segmentation.

- ☐ What would be the impact if a products Demand Segmentation Group changed due to a change in its Demand Patterns.

notes..............

notes..................

Chapter 13

Measuring Forecast Performance

Improving Forecast Accuracy is a key objective of the Demand Planner and it directly contributes to saving cash and increasing profitability for a company.

As you can see below, improving Forecast Accuracy can directly lead to improved customer service levels and reduce the need to maintain safety stocks to cover for the forecast error. This in turn releases cash and leads to indirect cost savings in multiple areas. Of course there are other factors that affect the costs and savings on the supply side but improving Forecast Accuracy is the most visible way to kick start efforts in this area.

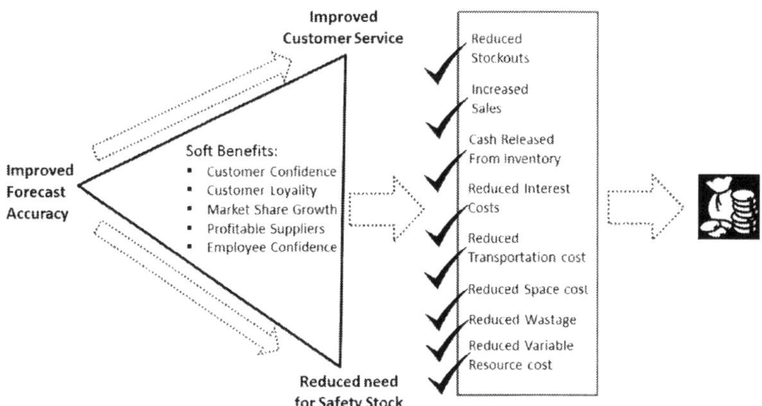

Forecast Performance Measurement is the whole activity of measuring various aspects of your Forecast (and Forecasting Process) to identify improvement areas and to track the performance of your Forecast over a period of time. In most cases these are measured using KPIs which reflect the performance of the Demand Planning as well as the wider supply chain planning teams.

Key Factors affecting Forecast Performance

Measuring Forecast Performance involves a few key decisions to be made upfront to ensure there is a standardised set of rules governing them. This is especially important if there are multiple teams or countries within your organization, and Forecast Performance needs to be compared among them to identify the ones working best. The following are factors that are typically considered while drafting a set of standard ways of measurement:

Forecast Components: We need to keep in mind that when we measure our Forecast Performance, we are actually measuring the performance of our Forecasting Algorithm based on Planner decided parameters, plus any modification made by the Planner in terms of Market Intelligence / External Input. This means that the planner has an equally important role, if not bigger, as the Forecasting Algorithm used. Most systems these days allow the Forecast to be stored as its components which enables you to separately measure the performance of your statistical forecast as well as the Market Intelligence and Total Forecast. It's best to decide upfront as to what components will be measured and their purpose so that the right granularity of data is stored in history. For Example Statistical Forecast Performance may be measured to drive fine-tuning of Algorithm Parameters while the Market Intelligence and Total Forecast may be measured to see the impact of Planner changes and the overall Bias of your planning teams.

Frequency: This defines how frequently Forecast Performance will be measured. It's common to have Forecast Performance measured in the same time Frequency that you have your Forecasting Time Buckets. However in some cases you may want to have more granular measurement. For example, you may be forecasting in weekly buckets and measuring performance in weekly buckets, but in case of major promotions you may want to track and measure performance on a daily basis for the current week to track the performance of the promotion and take corrective actions mid-week if required. Some of these promotions may run only for one or a few weeks and waiting till the end of the week to measure how we performed will be too late.

Levels: Forecast Performance can be measured at different levels. In fact companies will usually measure the performance at more than one level depending upon the objective and audience. SKU level Forecast Performance and Error may be used for computing statistical safety stock requirements at DCs while aggregate category or brand level performance may be used for S&OP and mid-term planning.

Lags: Forecast Lags describe how much in advance of a time period was the forecast made. This defines the distance between the Forecaster and the Forecasted Period. In the example below, Week 0 indicates the current planning week and Week 1 to Week 6 are the next forecast periods for a SKU. The planner finalises the forecast numbers in the first line and publishes it in Week 0. We then move to week 1 and the planner can potentially reforecast the same SKU with different numbers for Week 2 to Week 6. This goes on and we see him making changes when he is week2 and week3 as well.

Forecasted In	Week 1	Week 2	Week 3	Week 4	Week 5	Week 6
Week0	100	80	120	**140**	90	100
Week1		100	100	**120**	120	100
Week2			100	**80**	100	120
Week3				**100**	120	80

Now, if we look at Week 4, we potentially have four different forecasted numbers for the same periods which could result in different forecast errors and accuracy. If the Actual sale that happens in week 4 is 100, what should the forecast accuracy be taken as?

Let's look at the column headed Week4, in this case the forecast of 100 made in week 3 is known as Lag 1 Forecast (as that's the closest to the actual week) , Lag 2 Forecast is 80 , Lag 3 Forecast is 120 and so on.

Companies frequently store multiple lags of forecast and compare accuracy at different lags for different business purposes. The Lags used are also impacted by your supply and delivery lead times. For example, it's no point measuring a Lag 1 Forecast if your supply or delivery lead time is 2 weeks as the company has no chance of responding to any Forecast change at the last moment.

Usage: Different Lags may be used for measuring Forecast performance at different planning stages. For example:

Lag 0	Promotions Tracking within the week
Lag 1	Forecast Accuracy for Weekly Total Forecast
Lag 2	Forecast Accuracy of Final Promotions Uplifts
Lag 3	S&OP Plans Performance
Lag 4	S&OP Plans Performance
Lag 8 & 12	Supply & Manufacturing Impact
Lag 52	Annual Plans Performance

As we can see there can be multiple lags used for different purposes, but care needs to be taken to ensure that only the ones needed by the business are used. As the number of lags stored increases, there can be a rapid increase in the amount of data stored leading to non-value added reporting activity and impact on systems performance. Note : Some companies indicate lags counting backwards from week 0, in this case Lag 1 becomes Week minus 1 (WK-1 or W-1) , Lag 2 becomes Week minus 2 (WK-2 or W-2) and so on.

Review: Apart from S&OP Meetings, there needs to be a formal framework for reviewing the Forecast Performance to continuously drive improvement to the forecasting process. Performance reports should be published to all stakeholders regularly and the performance metrics be linked to individual planner targets.

Forecasting Metrics and KPIs

There are a number of metrics and Key Performance Indicators used by different companies, and each company needs to decide their own set of KPIs depending on their business needs. The key point is to make them consistent across business units and across time so that you can compare the performance across time as well as across different teams. Some of the main KPIs used are given below with simple calculations for conceptual understanding:

Error: The Forecast Error is the difference between the Historical Actual Value (of sales or the value being forecasted) and its Forecasted Value for the same Period. Note that a single historical period can have multiple Forecast Error Values depending on the Lag of the Forecast being used. You will recollect that the Lag defines how far in advance the forecast was generated.

Historical Actual Sale	30	40	70	60	80	100
Historical Forecast	10	35	60	60	45	110
Error	20	5	10	0	35	-10

Mean Error: As the Forecast Error is computed individually for each period, we can use it to track performance period after period. However, to get a single number measure of Error for a SKU we need to consolidate these individual errors into a SKU level single metric. One Metric used for this is Mean Error, which is the average of all the errors (sum of all errors / number of periods)

							Mean Error
Historical Actual Sale	30	40	70	60	80	100	
Historical Forecast	10	35	60	60	45	110	
Error	20	5	10	0	35	-10	10

A positive Mean Error indicates that the SKU is being underforecasted across the periods while a negative Mean Error indicates its being overforecasted. The greater the difference of the Mean Error from zero the worse is the forecast.

MSE and MAD: Mean Error is however not a very useful statistic as the positive and negative errors can cancel each other out in the mean calculation, which can be misleading. This can be seen in the example below:

							Mean Error
Historical Actual Sale	30	40	70	60	80	100	
Historical Forecast	10	60	60	70	45	135	
Error	20	-20	10	-10	35	-35	0

A Mean Error of zero in this case can be misleading and does not reflect the high and low errors. There are two common Metrics, companies use to get around this issue.

The **Mean Squared Error (MSE)** is computed by taking the average of the squares of the error instead of the errors. This converts all the negative errors to positive when they are squared.

							Mean Error	MSE
Historical Actual Sale	30	40	70	60	80	100		
Historical Forecast	10	60	60	70	45	135		
Error	20	-20	10	-10	35	-35	0	
Squared Error	400	400	100	100	1225	1225		575

The **Mean Absolute Deviation (MAD)** achieves the same by taking absolute values of the error, which converts the negative to positive as well.

							Mean Error	MAD
Historical Actual Sale	30	40	70	60	80	100		
Historical Forecast	10	60	60	70	45	135		
Error	20	-20	10	-10	35	-35	0	
Absolute Deviation	20	20	10	10	35	35		21.67

MSE suffers from a drawback due to the fact that it weights bigger errors and outliers more heavily due to the numbers being squared. This means that any SKU with an outlier will usually show a higher MSE than another SKU that may be worse overall but have no big outliers.

MSE is also not in the same units as the units being forecasted as the errors have been squared. To bring the MSE down to the same unit we have to perform an additional step of taking the square root of MSE (called Root MSE or RMSE)

MAPE : Mean Absolute Percentage Error or MAPE represents the average deviation or error as a percentage of the Historical Actual for a SKU. Its simply the deviations taken as a percentage each period and then averaged.

							Mean Error	MAPE
Historical Actual Sale	30	40	70	60	80	100		
Historical Forecast	10	60	60	70	45	135		
Error	20	-20	10	-10	35	-35	0	
Absolute Deviation	20	20	10	10	35	35		
Absolute % Deviation	67	50	14	17	44	35		37.73

While MAPE may look like a useful metric that could be used to convey the average error without involving volumes, it has some drawbacks. In cases where the Historical Actuals are very low the percentages can become huge and make the MAPE calculated unrealistic. This is because the error is computed as a percentage of the Historical Actual. See the example below where a single low actual value for period 2 changes the MAPE drastically:

							Mean Error	MAPE
Historical Actual Sale	30	3	70	60	80	100		
Historical Forecast	10	60	60	70	45	135		
Error	20	-57	10	-10	35	-35	-6.17	
Absolute Deviation	20	57	10	10	35	35		
Absolute Deviation as % of Actual	66.7	1900	14	17	44	35		346.06

SMAPE : Symmetric MAPE uses the average of Actual and Forecast for computing the absolute percentage deviation. SMAPE has the property of self limiting the error to a maximum of 200 and reduces the impact of low Historical Actuals and outliers.

							Mean Error	SMAPE
Historical Actual Sale	30	3	70	60	80	100		
Historical Forecast	10	60	60	70	45	135		
Error (Forecast-Actual)	20	-57	10	-10	35	-35	-6.17	
Absolute Deviation	20	57	10	10	35	35		
(Forecast + Actual)/2	20	31.5	65	65	63	118		
Absolute Deviation as % of (Forecast + Actual)/2	100	181	15	15	56	29.8		66.25

BIAS: A criteria for a good Forecast is that it is not Biased. Forecast BIAS reflects any consistent overforecasting or underforecasting for a SKU. This has an impact of causing excess inventory to build up during the overforecasting period and to cause stockouts during the underforecasted periods as the issues caused by one periods forecast are not adjusted in the subsequent periods. Usually this is also a strong indicator that either your Forecasting Model, or your rules and parameters for the SKU, need to be revisited. Its also good practice to flag/measure Bias only when its consistent over a longer duration of time (usual practice being 8 weeks or 13 weeks). Any periods shorter could be a blip due to a buildup for promotions or peak period.

							Mean Error
Historical Actual Sale	30	40	70	60	80	100	
Historical Forecast	10	35	60	60	45	110	
Error	20	5	10	10	35	-10	11.67
+ or - Bias	1	1	1	1	1	-1	
Tracking Signal	1	2	3	4	5	1	

In the example above the forecast has a positive Bias and we can see the forecast has been consistently been overforecasted for 5 weeks.

Sample Format Monthly Performance Tracking

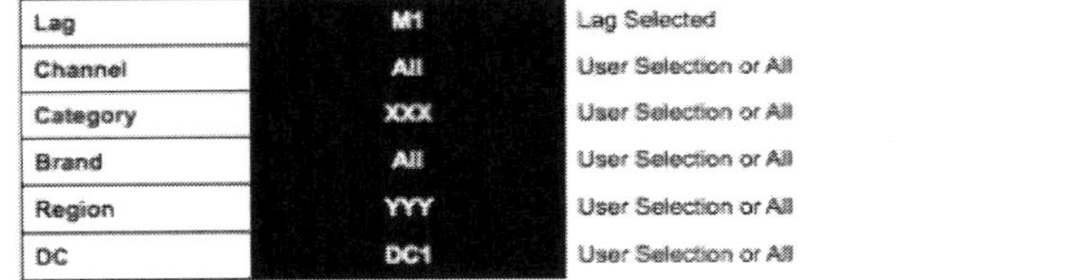

Lag	M1	Lag Selected
Channel	All	User Selection or All
Category	XXX	User Selection or All
Brand	All	User Selection or All
Region	YYY	User Selection or All
DC	DC1	User Selection or All

Item	Description	MAA	May	June	July	August	Sept	Oct	Nov	Dec	Jan	Feb	March	April
1001	Item 1	92.0%	92.0%	89.7%	92.5%	79.0%	89.3%	93.3%	94.2%	89.6%	97.5%	97.4%	97.9%	
1002	Item 2	92.0%	92.0%	89.7%	92.5%	79.0%	89.3%	93.3%	94.2%	89.6%	97.5%	97.4%	97.9%	
1003	Item 3	92.0%	92.0%	89.7%	92.5%	79.0%	89.3%	93.3%	94.2%	89.6%	97.5%	97.4%	97.9%	
1004	Item 4	92.0%	92.0%	89.7%	92.5%	79.0%	89.3%	93.3%	94.2%	89.6%	97.5%	97.4%	97.9%	
1005	Item 5	92.0%	92.0%	89.7%	92.5%	79.0%	89.3%	93.3%	94.2%	89.6%	97.5%	97.4%	97.9%	
	Total													

Avg of 12 months

Rolling 12 calendar Months Data backwards from current month

Sample Format for Weekly Performance Tracking

Channel	All	User Selection or All
Category	XXX	User Selection or All
Brand	All	User Selection or All
Region	YYY	User Selection or All
DC	DC1	User Selection or All

Item	Description	Sales WK-4	Sales WK-3	Sales Wk-2	Sales Wk-1	%AbsErr WK-4	%AbsErr WK-3	%AbsErr WK-2	%AbsErr WK-1	MAPE	Forecast Accuracy WK4	Forecast Accuracy WK3	Forecast Accuracy WK2	Forecast Accuracy WK1	4Week Avg Accuracy	4 Week Avg BIAS	BIAS SIGNAL
		UNIT	UNIT	UNIT	UNIT	%age	%age	%age	%age	%age	%age	%age	%age	%age	%age	UNIT	N/A
1002	Item 2	80	60	40	80	100%	100%	100%	100%	100%	0%	0%	0%	0%	0%	15	4.00
1003	Item 3	120	120	100	90	100%	100%	100%	100%	100%	0%	0%	0%	0%	0%	-52.5	-4.00
1004	Item 4	360	400	350	450	100%	100%	100%	100%	100%	0%	0%	0%	0%	0%	-90	-4.00
1005	Item 5	140	150	120	130	100%	100%	100%	100%	100%	0%	0%	0%	0%	0%	-7.5	-1.71
	Total	40	20	30	40	100%	100%	100%	100%	100%	0%	0%	0%	0%	0%	-2.5	-1.33

Thought Points ....

- [ ] What is the importance of measuring historical forecast performance. How would it help you improve your future forecast?
- [ ] How can improving your forecast performance help your company?
- [ ] How frequently do you think forecast performance should be measured. What are the factors that drive this.

notes.............

notes……………

notes.................

Printed in Great Britain
by Amazon